Betty Crocker's
VEGETARIAN COOKING

PRENTICE HALL

New York   London   Toronto   Sydney   Tokyo   Singapore

MACMILLAN

A Simon & Schuster Macmillan Company
1633 Broadway
New York, NY 10019

Copyright © 1994 by General Mills, Inc., Minneapolis, Minnesota

Library of Congress Cataloging-in-Publication Data

Crocker, Betty.
    [Vegetarian cooking]
    Betty Crocker's vegetarian cooking.
        p.   cm.
    Includes index.
    ISBN 0-671-88770-X
    1. Vegetarian cookery.   I. Title.   II. Title: Vegetarian
cooking.
    TX837.C8   1994
    641.5'636—dc20   93-36694
                                                            CIP

Designed by Levavi & Levavi

Manufactured in the United States of America

10   9   8   7   6   5   4   3

First Edition

CONTENTS

INTRODUCTION

Today, for a variety of reasons, more and more people are becoming interested in eating vegetarian meals. Some would like to reduce the amount of meat they eat, but not eliminate it completely. If this is your interest, you'll find cooking a few vegetarian meals a week is easy and delicious with the great recipes here.

If you'd like to eat vegetarian meals every day, we know you'll find the inspiration to help plan a vegetarian diet with these creative, enticing recipes. You'll enjoy the section on main dish soups and salads, great for supper at home, or to brown bag to work. Sample African Vegetable Stew, Gorgonzola-White Bean Soup or Indonesian Salad.

Looking for everyday skillet meals? Then turn to Satisfying Skillet Dinners and try Blue Cheese Omelet with Pears, Indian Spiced Lentils or Vermicelli with Lemony Green Vegetables. And when you'd like the convenience of a casserole, you can cook Cheese Manicotti, Ricotta Cheese Enchiladas, or Bulgur-Walnut Casserole.

And finally, we have a chapter called Pizzas, Sandwiches and More, that showcases fresh pizza ideas, casual sandwiches and other delightful recipes. You'll love the individual Pita Pizzas and the wholesome Whole Wheat Ratatouille Calzone, and look forward to trying the Fruit Chimichangas.

With a complete guide to grains, a comprehensive cooking chart for both grains and rice, and more than 100 delectable recipes, you'll find this book makes cooking vegetarian meals a true treat.

THE BETTY CROCKER EDITORS

Vegetarian Basics

As you begin to make more vegetarian meals, you'll find information about grains and rice to be invaluable. We have included a glossary of grains, as well as a useful cooking chart for both rice and grains to give you confidence when buying and cooking grains and rice.

KNOW YOUR GRAINS

There are many grains available to us today in a variety of forms, from whole kernels to finely ground flours. Grains add color, texture and flavor to foods while providing benefits such as fiber. When they are combined with low-fat dairy products or beans, peas or lentils, they provide high-quality protein.

Grains vary in cooking time and water absorption, so follow package directions when making a recipe. (Ask for cooking directions if you buy your grains in bulk.) Use any leftover cooked grains in place of some of the meat in a casserole, mixed with cooked vegetables for a side dish or tossed into a salad.

Barley was one of the first grains ever cultivated. Pearl barley is the most commonly available and has the hull, most of the bran and some of the germ removed to shorten cooking time. It contains vitamins B_3, B_1 and potassium.

One cup of cooked barley provides the same amount of protein as a glass of milk.

Buckwheat kernels (groats) are hulled seeds of the buckwheat plant. Technically a fruit, it is used as a grain. Roasted groats are often called *kasha*. Buckwheat contains phosphorus, iron, potassium, vitamin E and B vitamins. It has a pungent flavor that can be overpowering. Buckwheat flour is usually mixed with all-purpose flour for pastas, pancakes, muffins and quick breads.

Corn is sometimes forgotten as a grain because we usually eat it as a vegetable. Whole kernel corn adds a naturally sweet flavor and a crunchy texture to breads, main dishes and side dishes. Paired with legumes or small amounts of animal protein from dairy products or eggs, corn provides a complete source of protein.

Cornmeal is available in degerminated and whole-grain forms. As *degerminated* indicates, the germ and bran have been removed. This type is widely available at grocery stores. Stone-ground whole-grain cornmeal may be a little harder to come by. It contains the germ and the bran which give it more flavor, texture and fiber. Look for whole-grain cornmeal at health food stores or a local mill.

Flaxseed is a small, brown, teardrop-shaped seed used in small amounts as roughage in cereals and bread products.

Oats that we eat for breakfast as oatmeal are steamed and flattened groats (hulled oat kernels). They are available as either regular (old-fashioned), quick-cooking or instant. Regular and quick-cooking oats are often used interchangeably. If a recipe specifies just one, however, do not substitute the other—they have different absorption properties. Oats contribute fiber, vitamin B_1, phosphorus and magnesium to the diet.

Oat Bran is the broken husks of the oat kernels and is more easily digested than wheat bran. It can be used as hot cereal or as a baking and cooking ingredient and is a good source of soluble fiber.

Quinoa (keen-wa) was once the staple of the Inca Indians in Peru. It is a small grain with a soft crunch and can be used in any recipe calling for rice. Be sure to rinse well before using to remove the bitter-tasting, naturally occurring saponin (nature's insect repellent) that forms on the outside of the kernel. Quinoa provides B vitamins, calcium, iron, phosphorus and, unlike other grains, is a complete protein.

Brown Rice is unpolished, meaning the outer hull has been removed but the germ and bran layers have not been "polished" off. This gives it a nutlike flavor and chewier texture than white rice. It is also a good source of fiber and vitamin B_1.

Wild Rice is actually an aquatic grass native to North America. It is more expensive than other rices because of its limited supply. Stretch it by mixing with other rices or grains. Purchase less expensive packages of broken kernels, when you find them, and use in soups and quick breads. Wild rice contains fiber, B vitamins, iron, phosphorus, magnesium, calcium and zinc.

Rye is a dark, earthy-flavored grain from which

pumpernickel is made. Rye groats can be eaten as a cereal or used whole or cracked as a baking and cooking ingredient in casseroles, pilafs and breads. Rye is nutritionally similar to wheat.

Rye Flour is usually labeled "light" or "dark." The light flour has been sifted and has had most of the bran removed. Dark flour is sometimes referred to as pumpernickel flour. Although it is a very flavorful bread flour, it doesn't have much gluten and should be blended with wheat flour for baking.

Wheat Berries are hulled whole-grain wheat kernels that still have the bran and germ. Cooked wheat berries can be used like rice in salads and side dishes. Wheat provides B vitamins, vitamin E and complex carbohydrates. Combining wheat with legumes or dairy products provides a complete protein.

Wheat Bran is the tough outer layer of the wheat berry. It is available unprocessed in its raw form or toasted, which makes it easier to chew. Wheat bran is a rich source of insoluble fiber.

Wheat Bulgur is whole wheat that's been cooked, dried and then broken into coarse fragments. It's different from cracked wheat because it is precooked. Bulgur supplies phosphorus and potassium and also contains some iron and B_1 and B_2 vitamins.

Cracked Wheat is whole wheat kernels that have been dried and then cracked by coarse milling. Like bulgur, its precooked cousin, cracked wheat contains phosphorus, potassium, iron, vitamins B_1 and B_2.

Wheat Flour is available in several different forms. *Quick-mixing flour* is instantized all-purpose flour, which means it disperses instantly in cold liquids, resulting in smooth gravies, sauces and batters. *Cake flour* is milled from soft wheat, which has a weaker gluten structure, creating tender cakes with greater volume. *All-purpose flour* is either milled from hard winter wheat or a blend of hard and soft winter wheats to provide a flour that produces acceptable results in a wide range of baked products. *Bread flour* is milled from hard winter wheat, hard spring wheat or a combination of the two and provides the gluten structure needed in yeast breads. Quick-mixing, cake, all-purpose and bread flours don't contain the bran or the germ of wheat. *Whole wheat flour* is ground from the whole wheat kernel, usually from hard spring wheat, and contains the nutrients of whole wheat berries.

Wheat Germ is the flaked embryo of the berry. Because it's high in oil, it is usually toasted, to extend its shelf life. It has a nutty flavor and can be sprinkled over cereal or used in baked goods. It is a good source of vitamins B_1, B_3, B_2, potassium and zinc.

RICE AND GRAINS COOKING CHART

Rinse grains in water before cooking (except couscous), and be sure to use an extra-fine mesh strainer for small grains such as quinoa. Grains lose moisture with age, so you may find that you need more or less liquid than the recipe calls for. If all the liquid is absorbed but the grain isn't quite tender, add a little more liquid and cook longer. If it is tender but all the liquid hasn't been absorbed, just drain. Cooked grains can be covered and refrigerated for up to a week.

Type of Un-cooked Grain	Amount of Cooking Liquid	Method of Cooking (Using 2-Quart Saucepan with Lid)	Approximate Cooking Time	Approximate Yield
Brown Rice (1 cup)	2¾ cups	Heat rice and liquid to a boil. Reduce heat. Cover and simmer.	45 to 50 minutes	4 cups
Regular Rice (1 cup)	2 cups	Heat rice and liquid to a boil. Reduce heat. Cover and simmer.	15 minutes	3 cups
Wild Rice (1 cup)	2½ cups	Heat rice and liquid to a boil. Reduce heat. Cover and simmer.	40 to 50 minutes	3 cups
Parboiled rice (converted) (1 cup)	2½ cups	Heat liquid to a boil. Stir in rice. Reduce heat. Cover and simmer.	20 minutes. Remove from heat. Let stand covered 5 minutes.	3 to 4 cups

(continued)

Rice and Grains Cooking Chart (*Continued*)

See general cooking instructions on page 7.

Type of Un-cooked Grain	Amount of Cooking Liquid	Method of Cooking (Using 2-Quart Saucepan with Lid)	Approximate Cooking Time	Approximate Yield
Precooked White Rice (instant) (1 cup)	1 cup	Heat liquid to a boil. Stir in rice. Cover and remove from heat.	Let stand covered 5 minutes.	2 cups
Precooked Brown Rice (instant) (1 cup)	1¼ cups	Heat liquid to a boil. Stir in rice. Reduce heat. Cover and simmer.	10 minutes	2 cups
Barley (regular) (1 cup)	4 cups	Heat liquid to a boil. Stir in barley. Reduce heat. Cover and simmer.	45 to 50 minutes. Let stand covered 5 minutes.	4 cups
Barley (quick-cooking) (1 cup)	2 cups	Heat liquid to a boil. Stir in barley. Reduce heat. Cover and simmer.	10 to 12 minutes. Let stand covered 5 minutes.	3 cups
Bulgur (1 cup)	3 cups	Pour boiling liquid over bulgur and soak. Do not cook.	Soak 30 to 60 minutes.	3 cups
Couscous (1 cup)	1½ cups	Heat liquid to a boil. Stir in couscous. Cover and remove from heat.	Let stand covered 5 minutes.	3 to 3½ cups
Kasha (roasted buckwheat kernels) (1 cup)	2 cups	Pour boiling liquid over kasha and soak. Do not cook.	Soak 10 to 15 minutes.	4 cups

Type of Un-cooked Grain	Amount of Cooking Liquid	Method of Cooking (Using 2-Quart Sauce-pan with Lid)	Approximate Cooking Time	Approximate Yield
Quinoa (1 cup)	2 cups	Heat quinoa and liquid to a boil. Reduce heat. Cover and simmer.	15 minutes	3 to 4 cups
Wheat Berries (1 cup)	2½ cups	Heat wheat berries and liquid to a boil. Reduce heat. Cover and simmer.	50 to 60 minutes	2¾ to 3 cups

HOW TO USE NUTRITION INFORMATION

Nutrition Information per serving for each recipe includes the amounts of calories, protein, carbohydrate, fat, cholesterol and sodium.

- If ingredient choices are given, the first listed ingredient is used in recipe nutrition information calculations.

- When ingredient ranges or more than one serving size is indicated, the first weight or serving is used to calculate nutrition information.

- "If desired" ingredients and recipe variations are not included in nutrition information calculations.

MENUS

Workday Dinner
Moroccan Garbanzo Beans with Raisins
(page 42)
Basmati or White Rice
Sliced Cucumbers with Dressing
Angelfood Cake

Easy Brunch
Mexican Strata (page 75)
Sliced Melon
Muffins
Sangria or Fruit Juice
Coffee and Tea

Pizza Night
Vegetable Pizza with Wheat Germ Crust
(page 82)
Tossed Salad
Beer or Cider
Fresh Fruit and Cookies

Summer Lunch
Gazpacho (page 15)
Brie and Cucumber on Rye (page 86)
Frozen Yogurt and Berries
Iced Tea

Winter Dinner
Vegetable Lasagne (page 56)
Soft Bread Sticks
Broccoli Sauteed with Garlic
Apple or Pear Crisp
Hot Chocolate

Company Dinner
Fettuccine with Wild Mushrooms (page 49)
Wheat Berry Salad (page 29)
Chilled Asparagus Spears
Sorbet or Sherbet with Chocolate or Fruit
Toppings

Lentil Vegetable Soup (page 19)

1

Hearty Soups and Salads

Finnish Summer Vegetable Soup

Try this fresh soup with rye bread and cheese.

2 cups water
2 small carrots, sliced
1 medium potato, cubed
¾ cup fresh or frozen green peas
1 cup cut fresh or frozen green beans
¼ small cauliflower, separated into flowerets
2 ounces fresh spinach, cut up (about 2 cups)
2 cups milk
2 tablespoons all-purpose flour
¼ cup whipping (heavy) cream
1½ teaspoons salt
⅛ teaspoon pepper
Chopped fresh dill weed or parsley (optional)

Heat water, carrots, potato, peas, beans and cauliflower to boiling in 3-quart saucepan; reduce heat. Cover and simmer until vegetables are almost tender, 10 to 15 minutes.

Add spinach; cook uncovered about 1 minute. Mix ¼ cup of the milk and the flour; stir gradually into vegetable mixture. Boil and stir 1 minute. Stir in remaining milk, the whipping cream, salt and pepper. Heat just until hot. Garnish each serving with dill weed. **10 servings**

PER SERVING: Calories 85; Protein 3 g; Carbohydrate 11 g; Fat 3 g; Cholesterol 10 mg; Sodium 380 mg

Tomato Vegetable Soup with Yogurt

The cold variation of this soup is just right for a hot-weather meal.

1 can (24 ounces) tomato juice (3 cups)
¼ to ½ teaspoon ground red pepper (cayenne)
¼ teaspoon salt
1 package (10 ounces) frozen whole kernel corn
1 bunch green onions (about 6), sliced
1 medium red or green pepper, coarsely chopped
1 medium zucchini, coarsely chopped
1 container (18 ounces) plain yogurt

Heat all ingredients except yogurt to boiling in 4-quart Dutch oven; reduce heat. Simmer uncovered, stirring occasionally, until vegetables are crisp-tender, 7 to 8 minutes. Remove from heat; cool 5 minutes before adding yogurt to prevent curdling.

Stir yogurt into soup until smooth. Heat over medium heat, stirring constantly, just until hot (do not boil). Garnish with chopped cilantro or parsley if desired. **4 servings**

COLD TOMATO VEGETABLE SOUP WITH YOGURT:
After stirring in yogurt, cover and refrigerate soup until chilled. Garnish with alfalfa sprouts if desired.

PER SERVING: Calories 200; Protein 11 g; Carbohydrate 35 g; Fat 2 g; Cholesterol 10 mg; Sodium 890 mg

French Cabbage Soup

3½ cups water
2 tablespoons margarine or butter
1 tablespoon vegetable or chicken bouillon granules
1 teaspoon Worcestershire sauce
¼ teaspoon pepper
2 medium onions, thinly sliced
2 medium carrots, shredded
1 small head green cabbage, shredded
1 clove garlic, finely chopped
6 slices French bread, toasted
1½ cups shredded Swiss cheese (6 ounces)
¼ cup grated Parmesan cheese

Heat all ingredients except bread and cheeses to boiling in 4-quart Dutch oven; reduce heat. Simmer uncovered, stirring occasionally, until vegetables are crisp-tender, 15 to 20 minutes.

Set oven control to broil. Pour soup into 6 oven-proof soup bowls or casseroles. Top each with 1 slice toast; sprinkle with Swiss and Parmesan cheeses. Broil soup with tops 3 to 4 inches from heat until cheese is melted and light brown, 1 to 2 minutes. **6 servings**

PER SERVING: Calories 275; Protein 13 g; Carbohydrate 27 g; Fat 13 g; Cholesterol 30 mg; Sodium 1010 mg

Gazpacho

This cold vegetable soup is native to both Spain and Latin America. Not all gazpachos feature tomatoes or bread, and some recipes call for a smooth puree of vegetables rather than crisp chunks.

4 slices bread, torn into pieces
4 large ripe tomatoes, chopped
2 medium cucumbers, chopped
1 medium green pepper, chopped
1 medium onion, chopped
1 cup water
¼ cup olive or vegetable oil
⅓ cup red wine vinegar
2 cloves garlic, finely chopped
2 teaspoons salt
1 teaspoon ground cumin
⅛ teaspoon pepper

Mix bread, three-quarters of the tomatoes, one-half of the cucumbers, one-quarter of the green pepper, one-half of the onion, the water and oil in large bowl. Cover and refrigerate 1 hour.

Place half the vegetable mixture in blender. Cover and blend on high speed 8 seconds. Repeat with remaining mixture. Stir in vinegar, garlic, salt, cumin and pepper. Cover and refrigerate at least 2 hours.

Place remaining chopped vegetables in small bowls. Cover and refrigerate; serve as accompaniments. **6 servings**

PER SERVING: Calories 185; Protein 3 g; Carbohydrate 15 g; Fat 12 g; Cholesterol 0 mg; Sodium 810 mg

African Vegetable Stew

Rice simmers along with the vegetables and broth in this delicious stew. A dollop of yogurt is a nice counterpoint to the richly seasoned broth.

1 cup chopped onion
½ cup chopped fresh parsley
2 cloves garlic, finely chopped
1 teaspoon ground cinnamon
½ teaspoon ground turmeric
¼ teaspoon pepper
¼ teaspoon ground ginger
2 tablespoons margarine or butter
5 cups water
1 cup sliced carrots
½ cup dried lentils
1 cup uncooked regular long grain rice
1 can (16 ounces) whole tomatoes (with liquid)
¾ teaspoon salt
1 package (10 ounces) frozen green peas
1 package (9 ounces) frozen sliced green beans
3 sprigs fresh mint, chopped
Plain yogurt

Cook and stir onion, parsley, garlic, cinnamon, turmeric, pepper and ginger in margarine in Dutch oven until onion is tender. Stir in water, carrots and lentils. Heat to boiling; reduce heat. Cover and cook 25 minutes.

Add rice, tomatoes and salt. Heat to boiling; reduce heat. Cover and cook 20 minutes. Stir in peas, green beans and mint. Heat to boiling; reduce heat. Cover and cook until peas and beans are tender, about 5 minutes. Serve with yogurt. **6 servings**

PER SERVING: Calories 320; Protein 12 g; Carbohydrate 57 g; Fat 5 g; Cholesterol 5 mg; Sodium 510 mg

Spicy Vegetable Stew

¾ cup chopped onion
1 clove garlic, finely chopped
2 tablespoons vegetable oil
1 large red bell pepper, cut into 2 × ½-inch strips
2 medium poblano or Anaheim chiles, seeded and cut into 2 × ½-inch strips
1 jalapeño chile, seeded and chopped
1 cup cubed Hubbard or acorn squash (about ½ pound)
2 cans (14½ ounces each) vegetable or chicken broth
½ teaspoon salt
½ teaspoon pepper
½ teaspoon ground coriander
1 cup thinly sliced zucchini (about 1 small)
1 cup thinly sliced yellow squash (about 1 small)
1 can (17 ounces) whole kernel corn, drained
1 can (16 ounces) pinto beans, drained

Cook onion and garlic in oil in Dutch oven over medium heat, stirring occasionally, until onion is tender. Stir in bell pepper, poblano and jalapeño chiles. Cook 15 minutes, stirring occasionally.

Stir in Hubbard squash, broth, salt, pepper and coriander. Heat to boiling; reduce heat. Cover and simmer about 15 minutes or until squash is tender. Stir in remaining ingredients. Cook uncovered about 10 minutes, stirring occasionally, until zucchini is tender. **6 servings**

PER SERVING: Calories 210; Protein 9 g; Carbohydrate 32 g; Fat 7 g; Cholesterol 0 mg; Sodium 960 mg

Italian Vegetable Soup

½ cup dried great northern, navy or kidney beans (about 4 ounces)
1 cup water
4 cups vegetable or chicken broth
2 small tomatoes, chopped (about 1 cup)
2 medium carrots, sliced (about 1 cup)
1 stalk celery, sliced (about ½ cup)
1 medium onion, chopped (about ½ cup)
1 clove garlic, chopped
½ cup uncooked macaroni
1 tablespoon chopped parsley
½ teaspoon salt
1½ teaspoons chopped fresh or ½ teaspoon dried basil leaves
⅛ teaspoon teaspoon pepper
1 bay leaf
¾ cup cut green beans
2 small zucchini, cut into 1-inch slices (about 2 cups)
Grated Parmesan cheese

Heat dried beans and water to boiling in Dutch oven. Boil uncovered 2 minutes; remove from heat. Cover and let stand 1 hour. (Add enough water to cover beans if necessary.) Heat to boiling; reduce heat. Cover and simmer 1 hour to 1 hour 30 minutes or until tender.

Add broth, tomatoes, carrots, celery, onion, garlic, macaroni, parsley, salt, basil, pepper and bay leaf to beans. Heat to boiling; reduce heat. Cover and simmer 15 minutes. Add green beans and zucchini. Heat to boiling; reduce heat. Cover and simmer 10 to 15 minutes or until macaroni and vegetables are tender. Remove bay leaf. Serve with cheese. **4 servings**

PER SERVING: Calories 195; Protein 13 g; Carbohydrate 29 g; Fat 4 g; Cholesterol 5 mg; Sodium 1320 mg

Cheddar Cheese Soup

After adding the shredded cheese, be careful not to let the mixture boil as it might separate.

  1 small onion, chopped
  1 medium stalk celery, thinly sliced
  2 tablespoons margarine or butter
  2 tablespoons all-purpose flour
  ¼ teaspoon pepper
  ¼ teaspoon dry mustard
  1 can (10¾ ounces) vegetable or chicken broth
  1 cup milk
  2 cups shredded Cheddar cheese (8 ounces)
  Paprika

Cover and simmer onion and celery in margarine in 2-quart saucepan until onion is tender, about 5 minutes. Stir in flour, pepper and mustard. Cook over low heat, stirring constantly, until smooth and bubbly; remove from heat. Add broth and milk. Heat to boiling over medium heat, stirring constantly. Boil and stir 1 minute. Stir in cheese; heat over low heat, stirring occasionally, just until cheese is melted. Sprinkle with paprika. **4 servings**

PER SERVING: Calories 340; Protein 18 g; Carbohydrate 9 g; Fat 26 g; Cholesterol 65 mg; Sodium 750 mg

Gorgonzola–White Bean Soup

One of Italy's premier cheeses teams with one of its favorite beans. Gorgonzola tastes to some like a strong Danish blue cheese: It makes a smooth, rich-tasting soup.

  ½ cup chopped onion (about 1 medium)
  ½ cup chopped celery (about 1 medium stalk)
  ½ cup chopped carrot (about 1 medium)
  1 tablespoon reduced-calorie margarine
  3 cups vegetable or chicken broth
  1 cup ¼-inch leek slices (about 1 medium)
  ½ cup dried white beans (about 4 ounces)
  1 cup skim milk
  1 ounce Gorgonzola cheese, crumbled

Cook onion, celery and carrot in margarine in 3-quart nonstick saucepan over medium heat until onion is tender, about 3 minutes. Stir in broth, leek and beans. Heat to boiling; boil 2 minutes. Reduce heat and simmer until beans are tender, about 2 hours. (Add water during cooking if liquid does not cover beans.) Stir in milk.

Place 1 cup of the soup in blender or food processor. Cover and blend on high speed, or process, until of uniform consistency, about 30 seconds; stir into remaining soup mixture. Stir in cheese until melted. **4 servings**

PER SERVING: Calories 155; Protein 7 g; Carbohydrate 20 g; Fat 5 g; Cholesterol 10 mg; Sodium 1380 mg

Hearty Bean and Pasta Stew

1 cup coarsely chopped tomato (about 1 large)
¾ cup uncooked macaroni shells
¼ cup chopped onion (about 1 small)
¼ cup chopped green bell pepper (about ½ small)
1 tablespoon chopped fresh or 1 teaspoon dried basil leaves
1 teaspoon Worcestershire sauce
1 clove garlic, finely chopped
1 can (16 ounces) kidney beans, drained
1 can (8 ounces) garbanzo beans, drained
1 can (14½ ounces) vegetable or chicken broth

Mix all ingredients in 2-quart saucepan. Heat to boiling, stirring occasionally; reduce heat. Cover and simmer about 15 minutes, stirring occasionally, until macaroni is tender. **4 servings**

PER SERVING: Calories 350; Protein 20 g; Carbohydrate 59 g; Fat 4 g; Cholesterol 0 mg; Sodium 760 mg

Dried Beans

The foaming and boiling over that is often attendant on the preparation of dried beans can be avoided. Add a tablespoon of margarine to the beans during their first cooking; if the water in which they are cooking is exceptionally hard, add approximately ¼ teaspoon baking soda per cup of beans as well.

Southwestern Bean Soup

1 medium onion, sliced
1 large clove garlic, crushed
2 tablespoons margarine or butter
1 tablespoon chile powder
¼ teaspoon ground coriander
1 can (28 ounces) whole tomatoes, undrained
1 can (20 ounces) kidney beans, drained
1 can (16 ounces) pinto beans, drained
1 can (4 ounces) chopped green chiles, drained
¼ cup shredded Cheddar cheese (2 ounces)
1 cup shredded Monterey Jack cheese (4 ounces)

Cook and stir onion and garlic in margarine in 3-quart saucepan over medium heat until onion is tender, about 5 minutes. Stir in remaining ingredients except cheeses; break up tomatoes. Heat to boiling; reduce heat. Cover and simmer 30 minutes.

Stir in Cheddar cheese and ½ cup of the Monterey Jack cheese; heat over low heat, stirring occasionally, just until cheese is melted. Sprinkle each serving with remaining Monterey Jack cheese. **6 servings**

MICROWAVE DIRECTIONS: Place onion, garlic and margarine in 3-quart microwavable casserole. Cover tightly and microwave on high until onion is tender, 2 to 4 minutes. Stir in remaining ingredients except cheeses; break up tomatoes. Cover tightly and microwave 10 minutes; stir.

Cover tightly and microwave until hot and bubbly, 6 to 9 minutes longer. Stir in Cheddar cheese and ½ cup of the Monterey Jack cheese. Cover tightly and let stand until cheese is melted, about 5 minutes. Sprinkle each serving with remaining Monterey Jack cheese.

PER SERVING: Calories 360; Protein 19 g; Carbohydrate 40 g; Fat 14 g; Cholesterol 30 mg; Sodium 910 mg

Lentil Vegetable Soup

1 cup chopped onion (about 1 large)
2 teaspoons chile powder
1 teaspoon salt
1 teaspoon ground cumin
2 cloves garlic, finely chopped
1 can (6 ounces) spicy tomato juice
3 cups water
1 cup dried lentils (about 6 ounces)
1 can (14½ ounces) whole tomatoes, undrained
1 can (4 ounces) chopped green chiles, undrained
1 cup fresh or frozen whole kernel corn
2 cups julienne strips zucchini (about 2 small)

Heat onion, chile powder, salt, cumin, garlic and tomato juice to boiling in 3-quart saucepan; reduce heat. Cover and simmer 5 minutes. Stir in remaining ingredients except corn and zucchini. Heat to boiling; reduce heat. Cover and simmer 20 minutes. Stir in corn; cover and simmer 10 minutes. Stir in zucchini; cover and simmer about 5 minutes or until lentils and zucchini are tender. **6 servings**

PER SERVING: Calories 165; Protein 11 g; Carbohydrate 32 g; Fat 1 g; Cholesterol 0 mg; Sodium 590 mg

Middle Eastern Stew

Lentils are an inexpensive—and fat-free—source of protein.

3 cups water
1¼ cups dried lentils (about 8 ounces)
2 cups 1-inch cubes potatoes (about 2 medium)
½ cup chopped onion (about 1 medium)
½ cup chopped celery (about 1 stalk)
1 tablespoon finely chopped parsley
1 tablespoon vegetable bouillon granules
1 teaspoon salt
1 teaspoon ground cumin
2 cloves garlic, finely chopped
2 cups ½-inch slices zucchini (about 2 medium)
Lemon wedges

Heat water and lentils to boiling in non-stick 4-quart Dutch oven; reduce heat. Cover and cook about 30 minutes or until lentils are almost tender.

Stir in remaining ingredients except zucchini and lemon wedges. Cover and cook about 20 minutes or until potatoes are tender. Stir in zucchini. Cover and cook 10 to 15 minutes or until zucchini is tender. Serve with lemon wedges. **6 servings**

PER SERVING: Calories 210; Protein 12 g; Carbohydrate 39 g; Fat 1 g; Cholesterol 0 mg; Sodium 1080 mg

Lentil Soup with Asparagus and Gruyère

4 cups water
1 cup dried lentils
1 tablespoon vegetable or chicken bouil-
    lon granules
½ teaspoon lemon pepper salt
1 small onion, chopped
1 stalk celery (with leaves), sliced
¾ pound fresh asparagus, cut into
    ½-inch pieces, or 1 package (10
    ounces) frozen asparagus cuts
1 cup shredded Gruyère or Swiss cheese
    (4 ounces)
Sour cream

Mix all ingredients except cheese and sour cream in 4-quart Dutch oven. Heat to boiling; reduce heat. Cover and simmer until lentils are very tender, about 45 minutes.

Remove 1 cup of the vegetables with slotted spoon; reserve. Carefully pour remaining hot mixture into blender or food processor. Cover and blend on high speed, or process, until smooth.

Mix processed mixture, reserved vegetables and the cheese in Dutch oven. Heat over medium heat, stirring constantly, until cheese is melted and mixture is hot. Garnish each serving with dollop of sour cream.   **6 servings**

PER SERVING: Calories 220; Protein 15 g; Carbohydrate 22 g; Fat 8 g; Cholesterol 25 mg; Sodium 810 mg

Tex-Mex Egg Salad

This very special egg salad turns the ho-hum into the highly delicious!

¼ cup reduced-calorie mayonnaise or
    salad dressing
¼ cup low-fat sour cream
¼ cup diced Monterey Jack cheese
    (1 ounce)
2 tablespoons chopped green onion
    (about 1 medium)
2 teaspoons chopped fresh cilantro or
    parsley
¼ teaspoon salt
4 hard-cooked eggs, chopped
1 jalapeño chile, seeded and finely
    chopped
4 medium tomatoes

Mix all ingredients except tomatoes. Cut stem ends from tomatoes. Place tomatoes cut sides down. Cut into sixths to within ½ inch of bottom. Carefully spread out sections. Spoon about ½ cup salad into each tomato.   **4 servings**

PER SERVING: Calories 205; Protein 10 g; Carbohydrate 9 g; Fat 14 g; Cholesterol 235 mg; Sodium 380 mg

Peruvian Potato Salad

1 small onion, thinly sliced and separated into rings
3 tablespoons lemon juice
½ teaspoon salt
⅛ teaspoon ground red pepper (cayenne)
1½ pounds new potatoes
2 packages (3 ounces each) cream cheese, softened and cut into ½-inch cubes
½ cup half-and-half
2 small serrano chiles, seeded and finely chopped
¼ teaspoon salt
¼ teaspoon ground turmeric
Bibb lettuce leaves
12 Greek olives
3 hard-cooked eggs, peeled and cut into fourths

Mix onion, lemon juice, ½ teaspoon salt and the red pepper; cover and reserve.

Heat 1 inch salted water (1 teaspoon salt to 1 cup water) to boiling. Add potatoes. Heat to boiling; reduce heat. Cover and cook until tender, 20 to 25 minutes; drain and cool. Peel potatoes; cut into fourths.

Heat cream cheese, half-and-half, chiles, ¼ teaspoon salt and the turmeric over low heat, stirring frequently, until mixture is smooth, 10 to 12 minutes.

Arrange potatoes on lettuce leaves. Spoon cheese mixture over potatoes. Drain onion; arrange on cheese and potatoes. Garnish with olives and eggs. **6 servings**

PER SERVING; Calories 290; Protein 9 g; Carbohydrate 28 g; Fat 16 g; Cholesterol 150 mg; Sodium 840 mg

Polish Salad with Pickled Eggs

The kitchens of Eastern Europe are famed for their hand with vinegars and the "warm" spices, among them cloves and allspice. This salad features pickled eggs, a striking magenta in color.

Pickled Eggs (below)
1 bunch leaf lettuce, torn into bite-size pieces
½ small red onion, thinly sliced and separated into rings
¼ cup olive or vegetable oil
2 tablespoons lemon juice
¼ teaspoon salt
Dash of pepper

Prepare Pickled Eggs. Toss lettuce and onion. Divide among 6 salad plates. Cut eggs into slices or fourths. Arrange 1 egg on top of each salad. Shake remaining ingredients in tightly covered container; drizzle over salads.

6 servings

Pickled Eggs

3 cups beet juice (cooking water from beets)
1 cup red wine vinegar
8 whole black peppercorns
4 whole allspice
4 whole cloves
1 bay leaf
6 hard-cooked eggs, peeled

Heat beet juice, vinegar, peppercorns, allspice, cloves and bay leaf to boiling; pour over eggs. Cover and refrigerate at least 24 hours.

PER SERVING: Calories 155; Protein 7 g; Carbohydrate 4 g; Fat 14 g; Cholesterol 210 mg; Sodium 240 mg

Indonesian Salad

Indonesian Salad

Coconut-Peanut Dressing (below)
1 cup bean sprouts
1 cup shredded cabbage
4 ounces tofu, drained and cut into
**   1-inch pieces**
2 tablespoons peanut or vegetable oil
1 cup sliced cooked potatoes
1 cup cooked cut green beans
1 cup cooked sliced carrots
1 medium cucumber, sliced
2 hard-cooked eggs, peeled and sliced

Prepare Coconut-Peanut Dressing. Pour enough boiling water over bean sprouts and cabbage to cover; let stand 2 minutes. Drain.

Cook tofu in oil in 10-inch skillet over medium heat, turning pieces gently, until light brown. Remove with slotted spoon; drain. Cook potatoes in same skillet until light brown; drain.

Arrange bean sprouts, cabbage, tofu, potatoes and remaining ingredients on platter. Pour dressing over salad. **6 servings**

Coconut-Peanut Dressing

½ cup flaked coconut
1 cup hot water
1 small onion, chopped
1 clove garlic, finely chopped
1½ teaspoons peanut oil or Ghee (right)
⅔ cup peanut butter
½ cup water
1 tablespoon sugar
½ teaspoon salt
¼ to ½ teaspoon chile powder
⅛ teaspoon ground ginger

Place coconut in blender; add 1 cup water. Cover and blend on high speed about 30 seconds.

Cook and stir onion and garlic in oil in 2-quart saucepan about 5 minutes. Stir in coconut and remaining ingredients. Heat to boiling, stirring constantly; reduce heat. Simmer uncovered, stirring occasionally, until slightly thickened, about 3 minutes. Serve warm.

Ghee

1 pound unsalted butter

Cut butter into pieces. Heat over low heat until melted. Increase heat to medium; heat to boiling. Immediately remove from heat and stir gently.

Return to heat; slowly heat to simmering. Simmer uncovered until butter separates into transparent substance on top and milk solids on bottom, 30 to 40 minutes. Remove from heat; let stand 5 minutes. Strain through cheesecloth into container. Cover and refrigerate no longer than 2 months.

PER SERVING: Calories 380; Protein 14 g; Carbohydrate 25 g; Fat 25 g; Cholesterol 70 mg; Sodium 380 mg

Greek Salad

Greek Salad

1 medium head lettuce, torn into bite-size
   pieces
1 bunch romaine, torn into bite-size
   pieces
1 cup crumbled feta or chèvre cheese
   (about 4 ounces)
24 Greek or green olives
10 radishes, sliced
1 medium cucumber, sliced
1 bunch green onions, cut into ½-inch
   pieces
1 carrot, shredded
Vinegar Dressing (below)

Toss lettuce and romaine. Arrange remaining ingredients except Vinegar Dressing on top. Serve with dressing. **6 servings**

Vinegar Dressing

½ cup olive or vegetable oil
⅓ cup wine vinegar
1 tablespoon chopped fresh or 1 teaspoon dried oregano leaves
1 teaspoon salt

Shake all ingredients in tightly covered container.

PER SERVING: Calories 280; Protein 5 g; Carbohydrate 9 g; Fat 25 g; Cholesterol 15 mg; Sodium 970 mg

Marinated Black-eyed Peas

This salad is a variation on the rustic Portuguese bean dishes popular around Lisbon. Marjoram is the expected herb, and we have added the fresh, citric punch of cilantro, too.

3 cups water
½ pound dried black-eyed peas (about
   1½ cups)
1 cup finely chopped onion
¼ cup chopped green pepper
¼ cup olive oil
2 tablespoons chopped fresh cilantro
2 tablespoons red wine vinegar
½ teaspoon salt
½ teaspoon dried marjoram leaves
¼ teaspoon pepper
2 cloves garlic, finely chopped
3 hard-cooked eggs, sliced

Heat water and peas to boiling in 3-quart saucepan. Boil 2 minutes; reduce heat. Cover and simmer until tender, 50 to 60 minutes; drain. Mix peas and remaining ingredients except 1 hard-cooked egg in large bowl. Cover and refrigerate 3 hours.

Arrange remaining egg on top of mixture; sprinkle with additional chopped cilantro if desired. **5 servings**

PER SERVING: Calories 320; Protein 14 g; Carbohydrate 32 g; Fat 15 g; Cholesterol 130 mg; Sodium 260 mg

Black Bean Salad

Black Bean Salad

Chile Dressing (below)
1 cup frozen whole kernel corn, rinsed to thaw and drained
1 cup diced jicama (about 5 ounces)
1 medium tomato, seeded and chopped (about ¾ cup)
2 green onions, sliced
2 cans (15 ounces each) black beans, rinsed and drained

Prepare Chile Dressing in large glass or plastic bowl. Stir in remaining ingredients.

4 servings

Chile Dressing

¼ cup red wine vinegar
2 tablespoons vegetable oil
½ teaspoon chile powder
¼ teaspoon ground cumin
1 small clove garlic, crushed

Shake all ingredients in tightly covered container.

PER SERVING: Calories 350; Protein 15 g; Carbohydrate 55 g; Fat 8 g; Cholesterol 0 mg; Sodium 380 mg

Caesar Bean Salad

1 can (16 ounces) great northern beans, drained
1 can (15½ ounces) red kidney beans, drained
1 can (15 ounces) garbanzo beans, drained
½ cup sweet pickle relish
½ cup Caesar dressing
¼ cup chopped fresh parsley
Salt and pepper to taste
Lemon wedges

Mix all ingredients except salt, pepper and lemon wedges in large bowl. Cover and refrigerate at least 1 hour, stirring occasionally.

Remove with slotted spoon and, if desired, arrange on salad greens; sprinkle with salt and pepper and, if desired, additional chopped parsley and grated Parmesan cheese. Garnish with lemon wedges.

5 servings

CAESAR BEAN SALAD WITH AVOCADOS: For each salad, place avocado half on salad plate. Spoon about ½ cup bean mixture onto avocado.

CAESAR BEAN SALAD WITH TOMATOES: For each salad, arrange 2 large slices tomato on salad plate. Spoon about ½ cup bean mixture onto tomato slices.

PER SERVING: Calories 450; Protein 17 g; Carbohydrate 59 g; Fat 16 g; Cholesterol 0 mg; Sodium 1090 mg

All Dressed Up

Head-start salad dressings take full advantage of prepared dressings but give them a hint of "homemade." You can add that personal touch with any of the following combinations for vegetable salads:

- ¼ cup oil-and-vinegar salad dressing and ¼ teaspoon chile powder

- ¼ cup oil-and-vinegar salad dressing and ¼ teaspoon dried oregano leaves

- ¼ cup oil-and-vinegar salad dressing and ¼ teaspoon ground savory

- ¼ cup oil-and-vinegar salad dressing and ¼ teaspoon dried thyme leaves

- ½ cup mayonnaise or salad dressing and ¼ cup catsup

- ½ cup mayonnaise or salad dressing, ¼ cup chili sauce, 1 drop red pepper sauce and dash of chile powder

Tortellini in Balsamic Vinaigrette

Tortellini in Balsamic Vinaigrette

A wonderful salad to make on a busy night.

1 package (7 ounces) uncooked tricolor cheese tortellini
Balsamic Vinaigrette (below)
2 cups broccoli flowerets
1 medium carrot, sliced
2 green onions, sliced

Cook tortellini as directed on package; drain. Rinse with cold water; drain.

Prepare Balsamic Vinaigrette in large bowl. Stir in remaining ingredients except tortellini. Stir in tortellini. **4 servings**

Balsamic Vinaigrette

¼ cup balsamic or cider vinegar
2 tablespoons olive or vegetable oil
1 tablespoon chopped fresh or 1 teaspoon dried basil leaves
¼ teaspoon paprika
⅛ teaspoon salt
1 clove garlic, crushed

Mix all ingredients.

PER SERVING: Calories 325; Protein 17 g; Carbohydrate 28 g; Fat 16 g; Cholesterol 140 mg; Sodium 550 mg

Wheat Berry Salad

Wheat berries are whole grains of wheat and can be found in health-food stores.

1 cup uncooked wheat berries
2½ cups water
1½ cups broccoli flowerets
½ cup chopped green onions
½ cup diced carrot (about 1 medium)
1 can (15 ounces) garbanzo beans, drained
Balsamic Dressing (below)

Heat wheat berries and water to boiling in 2-quart saucepan, stirring once or twice; reduce heat. Cover and simmer 50 to 60 minutes or until wheat berries are tender but still firm; drain. Toss wheat berries and remaining ingredients. Cover and refrigerate at least 1 hour.

4 servings

Balsamic Dressing

¼ cup balsamic or cider vinegar
2 tablespoons olive or vegetable oil
1 tablespoon chopped fresh or 1 teaspoon dried basil leaves
¼ teaspoon paprika
⅛ teaspoon salt
1 clove garlic, crushed

Shake all ingredients in tightly covered container.

PER SERVING: Calories 280; Protein 8 g; Carbohydrate 46 g; Fat 8 g; Cholesterol 0 mg; Sodium 300 mg

Minted Cottage Cheese Salad with Fruit

Minted Cottage Cheese Salad with Fruit

1 container (16 ounces) small curd
    creamed cottage cheese
1 tablespoon chopped fresh mint leaves
Lettuce leaves
1 cup blueberries, raspberries or
    blackberries
½ pint medium strawberries (about 1
    cup) or 1 large peach or nectarine,
    sliced
2 medium bananas, sliced
Coarsely chopped salted or toasted nuts
Ginger-Honey Dressing (below)

Mix cottage cheese and mint. Divide lettuce leaves among 4 salad plates. Spoon cheese mixture onto each. Arrange fruit on top; sprinkle with nuts. Serve with Ginger-Honey Dressing.

4 servings

Ginger-Honey Dressing

¼ cup vegetable oil
¼ cup lime juice
¼ cup honey
2 tablespoons mayonnaise or salad
    dressing
¼ teaspoon salt
¼ teaspoon ground ginger

Shake all ingredients in tightly covered container.

PER SERVING: Calories 520; Protein 17 g; Carbohydrate 45 g; Fat 30 g; Cholesterol 20 mg; Sodium 640 mg

Salad Savvy

There's a wide world of greens out there. Get to know them—they're the basics for a prize-winning salad bowl.

- Take lettuce for starters. Four main groups of its many varieties are commonly available: crisphead (notably iceberg); butterhead (including Boston and Bibb), with soft, pliable leaves; romaine (also called cos), with crisp, elongated dark leaves; and leaf lettuce (red or green), with tender "leafy" leaves that do not form heads.

- Store all greens in the refrigerator—in a covered container, a plastic bag or the crisper section. Watercress, parsley and fresh herbs, however, should always be refrigerated in large screwtop jars. These, as well as iceberg lettuce and romaine, will keep up to a week; most other greens will droop within a few days.

- Wash greens several hours before using—they need time to get crisp. Wash well under running cold water, then shake off the excess moisture. To remove remaining moisture, toss in a kitchen towel or pat dry. Return to the refrigerator.

Home-style Scrambled Eggs

2

Satisfying Skillet Dinners

---◻︎---

Home-style Scrambled Eggs

4 eggs
3 tablespoons water
½ teaspoon salt
2 tablespoons margarine or butter
3 tablespoons finely chopped onion
1 medium potato, cooked and cubed
(about 1 cup)
1 medium tomato, seeded and chopped
1 small zucchini, chopped

Beat eggs, water and salt with fork; set aside. Heat margarine in 10-inch skillet over medium heat until melted. Cook and stir vegetables in margarine 2 minutes. Pour egg mixture into skillet.

As mixture begins to set at bottom and side, gently lift cooked portions with spatula so that thin, uncooked portion can flow to bottom. Avoid constant stirring. Cook 3 to 5 minutes or until eggs are thickened throughout but still moist. **4 servings**

PER SERVING: Calories 175; Protein 7 g; Carbohydrate 12 g; Fat 11 g; Cholesterol 210 mg; Sodium 400 mg

Freezing Eggs

- Freeze egg whites in a plastic ice cube tray; remove to a plastic bag for storage. To measure, remember that 2 tablespoons of defrosted liquid egg white are equal to 1 fresh egg white. Thaw frozen egg whites in the refrigerator. Egg yolks require special treatment for freezing. If the yolks are to be used in scrambled eggs or egg pastry, add ⅛ teaspoon salt for each ¼ cup of egg yolks. If the yolks are to be used in custards or sweet sauces, add 1½ teaspoons sugar or 1½ teaspoons corn syrup for each ¼ cup of egg yolks.

- Hard-cooked egg yolks can be frozen successfully, but hard-cooked whites become tough and watery.

Tex-Mex Scrambled Eggs

6 corn tortillas (6-inch diameter)
3 tablespoons vegetable oil
½ cup chopped green onions
6 eggs, beaten
1 cup cubed Mexican-style process
    cheese spread with jalapeño chiles
    (about 4 ounces)
1 medium tomato, chopped

Cut each tortilla into 12 wedges. Heat oil in 10-inch skillet just until hot. Cook tortilla wedges in oil over medium-high heat, stirring frequently, until crisp; reduce heat. Add onions. Cook and stir over medium heat 1 minute.

Pour eggs over tortilla mixture. As eggs begin to set at bottom and side, gently lift cooked portions with spatula so that thin, uncooked portion can flow to bottom. Do not stir. Sprinkle with cheese. Cook 1 to 2 minutes longer or until cheese is melted and eggs are thickened throughout but still moist. Top with tomato. Sprinkle with chopped cilantro, oregano or parsley if desired. **4 servings**

PER SERVING: Calories 370; Protein 18 g; Carbohydrate 17 g; Fat 25 g; Cholesterol 410 mg; Sodium 555 mg

Onion Omelet with Tomatoes

Walnuts add wonderful flavor to this vegetable omelet.

1 tablespoon olive or vegetable oil
2 large onions, sliced
2 tablespoons chopped walnuts
4 eggs, separated
2 egg whites
¼ cup water
¼ teaspoon salt
2 cups chopped tomatoes (about 2 large)

Heat oven to 325°. Heat oil in 10-inch nonstick ovenproof skillet over medium heat. Cook onions in oil about 5 minutes, stirring frequently, until onions are light golden brown. Stir in walnuts.

Beat 6 egg whites, water and salt in large bowl on high speed until stiff but not dry. Beat 4 egg yolks on high speed about 3 minutes or until very thick and lemon colored. Fold into egg white mixture. Pour into skillet. Level surface gently; reduce heat to low. Cook about 5 minutes or until puffed and light brown on bottom. (Lift omelet carefully at edge to judge color.) Bake uncovered in oven 12 to 15 minutes or until knife inserted in center comes out clean. Tilt skillet; slip pancake turner or spatula under omelet to loosen. Invert onto warm platter; cut into wedges. Serve with chopped tomatoes. **4 servings**

PER SERVING: Calories 190; Protein 10 g; Carbohydrate 14 g; Fat 11 g; Cholesterol 215 mg; Sodium 240 mg

Mushroom Omelets

Mushroom Filling (below)
6 eggs
2 egg whites
⅓ cup water
½ teaspoon salt
⅛ teaspoon pepper
Vegetable oil

Prepare Mushroom Filling; keep warm. Mix remaining ingredients except oil just until egg whites and yolks are well blended. Lightly brush 8-inch nonstick omelet pan or skillet with oil; heat over medium-high heat until hot. For each omelet, quickly pour one-quarter of the egg mixture (about ½ cup) into pan. As eggs begin to set at bottom and side, gently lift cooked portions with spatula so that thin, uncooked portion can flow to bottom. Do not stir. When eggs are set but shiny, remove from heat. (Do not overcook—omelet will continue to cook after folding.) Spoon about ¼ cup Mushroom Filling on one side of omelet. Run spatula under unfilled side of omelet; lift over filling. Tilting pan slightly, turn omelet onto plate.   **4 servings**

Mushroom Filling

1 tablespoon reduced-calorie margarine
2 cups sliced mushrooms
1 large clove garlic, finely chopped
2 tablespoons chopped green onions
2 tablespoons chopped parsley
2 tablespoons grated Parmesan cheese

Heat margarine in 10-inch nonstick skillet over medium-high heat until hot. Stir in mushrooms, garlic and onions; cook and stir until moisture is evaporated, about 2 minutes. Remove from heat; stir in parsley and cheese.

PER SERVING: Calories 170; Protein 12 g; Carbohydrate 3 g; Fat 12 g; Cholesterol 410 mg; Sodium 480 mg

Blue Cheese Omelet with Pears

4 eggs
1 tablespoon margarine or butter
¼ cup crumbled Danish blue cheese or Gorgonzola cheese
1 tablespoon chopped fresh chives
1 unpeeled pear, cut into wedges

Mix eggs with fork just until whites and yolks are blended. Heat margarine in 8-inch skillet or omelet pan over medium-high heat just until margarine begins to brown. As margarine melts, tilt skillet to coat bottom completely.

Quickly pour eggs, all at once, into skillet. Slide skillet back and forth rapidly over heat and, at the same time, stir quickly with fork to spread eggs continuously over bottom of pan as they thicken. Let stand over heat a few seconds to lightly brown bottom of omelet. (Do not overcook—omelet will continue to cook after folding.)

Tilt skillet; run fork under edge of omelet, then jerk skillet sharply to loosen eggs from bottom of skillet. Sprinkle with blue cheese and chives. Fold portion of omelet nearest you just to center. (Allow for portion of omelet to slide up side of skillet.)

Grasp skillet handle; turn omelet onto warm plate, flipping folded portion of omelet over so far side is on bottom. Serve with pear wedges.   **2 servings**

PER SERVING: Calories 310; Protein 16 g; Carbohydrate 14 g; Fat 21 g; Cholesterol 440 mg; Sodium 430 mg

Malaysian Omelet

The peanut oil here will not brown excessively as butter and margarine often do with long cooking. You can serve this thin omelet in wedges, as Malaysians do.

2 cups mixed thinly sliced eggplant, green pepper and onion
1 tablespoon peanut oil
1 medium onion, finely chopped
1 green chile, seeded and finely chopped (about 1 tablespoon)
1 red chile, seeded and finely chopped (about 1 tablespoon)
1 clove garlic, finely chopped
2 tablespoons peanut oil
4 eggs, beaten
¼ teaspoon salt
¼ teaspoon pepper

Cook 2 cups vegetables in 1 tablespoon oil until tender; reserve.

Cook chopped onion, chiles and garlic in 2 tablespoons oil in 10-inch skillet until tender. Mix eggs, salt and pepper; pour into skillet. Cover and cook over low heat until eggs are set and light brown on bottom, about 8 minutes. Cut eggs into wedges; spoon reserved vegetable mixture over omelet.   **4 servings**

PER SERVING: Calories 195; Protein 7 g; Carbohydrate 8 g; Fat 15 g; Cholesterol 215 mg; Sodium 200 mg

Broccoli and Swiss Cheese Frittata

1 medium onion, chopped
2 cloves garlic, finely chopped
2 tablespoons margarine or butter
1 tablespoon olive or vegetable oil
1 package (10 ounces) frozen chopped broccoli, thawed and drained
8 eggs
½ teaspoon salt
¼ teaspoon pepper
1 cup shredded Swiss cheese (4 ounces)
1 to 2 tablespoons chopped fresh or 1 teaspoon dried oregano leaves
2 tablespoons shredded Swiss cheese

Cook onion and garlic in margarine and oil in 10-inch ovenproof skillet over medium heat, stirring frequently, until onion is tender, about 5 minutes. Remove from heat; stir in broccoli.

Beat eggs, salt and pepper until blended; stir in 1 cup cheese and the oregano. Pour over broccoli mixture. Cover and cook over medium-low heat until eggs are set around edge and light brown on bottom, 9 to 11 minutes.

Set oven control to broil. Broil frittata with top about 5 inches from heat until golden brown, about 2 minutes. Sprinkle with 2 tablespoons cheese; cut into wedges.   **6 servings**

PER SERVING: Calories 250; Protein 16 g; Carbohydrate 6 g; Fat 18 g; Cholesterol 300 mg; Sodium 370 mg

Zucchini Frittata

6 eggs
¼ cup water
3 tablespoons chopped parsley
2 tablespoons soft bread crumbs
1 teaspoon salt
1 clove garlic, finely chopped
1 tablespoon olive or vegetable oil
1 cup ¼-inch zucchini slices (about 1 medium)
Flour
1 tablespoon grated Parmesan cheese

Beat eggs, water, parsley, bread crumbs, salt and garlic. Heat oil in 8-inch nonstick ovenproof skillet over medium heat until hot. Coat zucchini lightly with flour; cook until golden, about 2 minutes on each side. Pour egg mixture over zucchini. Cook without stirring until eggs are thickened throughout but still moist, 3 to 5 minutes. Gently lift cooked portion with spatula so that thin, uncooked portion can flow to bottom. Sprinkle with cheese.

Set oven control to broil. Broil omelet with top 5 inches from heat until golden brown, 3 to 4 minutes. Loosen edge with spatula; slip cheese-side up onto serving plate. **3 servings**

PER SERVING: Calories 245; Protein 14 g; Carbohydrate 10 g; Fat 16 g; Cholesterol 550 mg; Sodium 930 mg

Egg Foo Yong

4 eggs
2 egg whites
1⅓ cups bean sprouts
¼ cup sliced green onions
¼ teaspoon salt
Vegetable oil
Brown Sauce (below)

Beat eggs and egg whites until thick and lemon colored, about 5 minutes. Stir in bean sprouts, onions and salt. For each patty, lightly brush 10-inch nonstick skillet with oil. Heat over medium heat until hot.

Pour scant ¼ cup egg mixture at a time into skillet. Push cooked egg up over bean sprouts with broad spatula to form a patty. Cook until patty is set; turn. Cook over medium heat until other side is brown. Place on warm platter; keep warm. Prepare Brown Sauce; serve with egg patties. **4 servings**

Brown Sauce

½ cup water
2 tablespoons soy sauce
1 teaspoon cornstarch
1 teaspoon sugar
1 teaspoon vinegar

Cook all ingredients until mixture thickens and boils, stirring constantly. Boil and stir 1 minute.

PER SERVING: Calories 115; Protein 9 g; Carbohydrate 4 g; Fat 7 g; Cholesterol 275 mg; Sodium 750 mg

Stir-fried Eggs with Mushrooms

The earthy flavor of dried mushrooms is nice here with the Chinese accents of green onion, fresh ginger, rice wine and soy sauce.

3 dried black Chinese mushrooms
2 tablespoons peanut oil
½ cup sliced green onions
1 teaspoon finely chopped gingerroot
½ cup sliced oyster mushrooms
6 eggs, beaten
2 tablespoons rice wine (sake) or vegetable broth
1 tablespoon soy sauce
Sesame oil

Cover black mushrooms with warm water; let stand 20 minutes. Drain and rinse. Remove and discard stems from mushrooms. Cut mushrooms into thin strips; reserve.

Heat peanut oil in 10-inch skillet or wok until hot. Cook onions and gingerroot until tender; stir in reserved black mushrooms and oyster mushrooms. Mix eggs, wine and soy sauce; pour into skillet. As mixture begins to set at bottom and side, gently lift cooked portions with spatula so that thin, uncooked portion can flow to bottom. Avoid constant stirring. Cook until eggs are thickened throughout but still moist, 3 to 5 minutes. Sprinkle with sesame oil; serve immediately.   **4 servings**

PER SERVING: Calories 210; Protein 10 g; Carbohydrate 6 g; Fat 16 g; Cholesterol 320 mg; Sodium 360 mg

Curried Eggs and Vegetables on Rice

For this dish, you make your own curry; commercial curries vary widely.

8 ounces small whole mushrooms
1 cup finely chopped onion (about 1 large)
1 tablespoon reduced-calorie margarine
1 teaspoon salt
1 teaspoon ground coriander
½ teaspoon ground turmeric
½ teaspoon ground ginger
½ teaspoon ground cumin
3 medium tomatoes, cut into wedges
¼ cup vegetable or chicken broth
6 hard-cooked eggs
1 teaspoon lemon juice
2 cups hot cooked rice

Cook and stir mushrooms and onion in margarine in 10-inch nonstick skillet until onion is tender, about 5 minutes. Stir in salt, coriander, turmeric, ginger and cumin; cook and stir 1 minute. Stir in tomatoes and broth. Heat to boiling; reduce heat. Simmer uncovered 5 minutes, stirring occasionally.

Cut eggs lengthwise in half. Carefully place eggs yolk-side up in skillet; spoon sauce over eggs. Simmer uncovered without stirring until eggs are hot, 3 to 5 minutes. Stir in lemon juice just before serving. Serve over rice.   **4 servings**

PER SERVING: Calories 305; Protein 14 g; Carbohydrate 37 g; Fat 11 g; Cholesterol 410 mg; Sodium 1170 mg

Herbed Eggs and Vegetables on Polenta

⅔ cup yellow cornmeal
½ cup cold water
2 cups boiling water
1 tablespoon chopped fresh or 1 teaspoon dried basil leaves
½ teaspoon salt
1 tablespoon reduced-calorie margarine
8 ounces small whole mushrooms
1 medium onion, sliced
1 medium red bell pepper, cut into strips
1 tablespoon chopped fresh or 1 teaspoon dried basil leaves
½ cup vegetable or chicken broth
2 teaspoons cornstarch
½ teaspoon salt
6 hard-cooked eggs, cut lengthwise into halves

Mix cornmeal and cold water in 2-quart nonstick saucepan. Stir in boiling water, 1 tablespoon basil and ½ teaspoon salt. Cook, stirring occasionally, until mixture thickens and boils; reduce heat to low. Cook about 10 minutes, stirring occasionally, until very thick; remove from heat. Keep warm.

Heat margarine in 10-inch nonstick skillet over medium heat. Cook mushrooms, onion, bell pepper and 1 tablespoon basil about 7 minutes, stirring occasionally, until onion is tender. Stir broth into cornstarch and ½ teaspoon salt. Stir into vegetable mixture. Heat to boiling, stirring occasionally. Boil and stir 1 minute; reduce heat.

Carefully stir eggs into vegetable mixture. Simmer uncovered 3 to 5 minutes, without stirring, until eggs are hot. Serve over polenta.

4 servings

PER SERVING: Calories 170; Protein 6 g; Carbohydrate 28 g; Fat 4 g; Cholesterol 55 mg; Sodium 700 mg

Eggs Florentine

1 package (10 ounces) frozen chopped spinach
Mornay Sauce (below)
4 Poached Eggs (below)
2 tablespoons grated Parmesan cheese
1 tablespoons dry bread crumbs

Cook spinach as directed on package; drain. Place spinach in ungreased shallow 1-quart baking dish; keep warm. Prepare Mornay Sauce and Poached Eggs. Place eggs on spinach. Cover with Mornay Sauce; sprinkle with cheese and bread crumbs. Set oven control to broil. Broil with top about 5 inches from heat until light brown, about 1 minute. **4 servings**

Mornay Sauce

2 teaspoons margarine or butter
2 teaspoons all-purpose flour
½ teaspoon vegetable or chicken bouillon granules
Dash of ground nutmeg
Dash of ground red pepper (cayenne)
¾ cup half-and-half
¼ cup shredded Swiss cheese

Heat margarine in 1-quart saucepan until melted. Blend in flour, bouillon granules, nutmeg and red pepper. Cook over low heat, stirring constantly, until mixture is smooth and bubbly. Stir in half-and-half. Heat to boiling, stirring constantly. Boil and stir 1 minute. Add cheese; stir until cheese is melted.

Poached Eggs

Heat water (1½ to 2 inches) to boiling; reduce to simmer. Break each egg into saucer; holding saucer close to water's surface, slip 1 egg at a time into water. Cook until of desired doneness, 3 to 5 minutes. Remove eggs from water.

PER SERVING: Calories 215; Protein 12 g; Carbohydrate 8 g; Fat 15 g; Cholesterol 240 mg; Sodium 400 mg

Savory Egg Pockets

Savory Egg Pockets

2 tablespoons margarine or butter
¼ cup chopped green bell pepper
1 small tomato, seeded and chopped
  (about ½ cup)
8 eggs
1 teaspoon Worcestershire sauce
¼ teaspoon salt
2 pita breads (6 inches in diameter), cut
  in half and opened to form pockets
½ cup alfalfa sprouts

Heat margarine in 10-inch skillet over medium heat until melted. Cook bell pepper and tomato in margarine about 3 minutes, stirring occasionally, until bell pepper is tender. Mix eggs, Worcestershire sauce and salt. Pour into skillet.

As mixture begins to set at bottom and side, gently lift cooked portions with spatula so that thin, uncooked portion can flow to bottom. Avoid constant stirring. Cook 3 to 5 minutes or until eggs are thickened throughout but still moist. Spoon into pita breads. Top with alfalfa sprouts. **4 servings**

PER SERVING: Calories 320; Protein 17 g; Carbohydrate 27 g; Fat 16 g; Cholesterol 430 mg; Sodium 540 mg

Garbanzo Beans and Vegetables

1 tablespoon olive or vegetable oil
1 medium onion, sliced
2 cloves garlic, finely chopped
2 cups sliced carrots
1 teaspoon ground coriander
1 teaspoon vegetable or chicken bouillon
  granules
½ teaspoon salt
¼ teaspoon ground turmeric
⅛ teaspoon ground red pepper (cayenne)
2 medium zucchini, sliced
1 can (15 ounces) garbanzo beans,
  undrained

Heat oil in 3-quart saucepan over medium-high heat. Sauté onion and garlic 3 minutes. Stir in remaining ingredients. Heat to boiling; reduce heat. Cover and simmer 12 to 15 minutes or until vegetables are crisp-tender. Serve over couscous. **4 servings**

Couscous

1¼ cups water
⅓ cup raisins
2 tablespoons margarine or butter
¼ teaspoon salt
¾ cup uncooked quick-cooking
  couscous

Heat water, raisins, margarine and salt to boiling in 1-quart saucepan. Stir in couscous; cover. Remove from heat and let stand covered 5 minutes.

PER SERVING: Calories 440; Protein 13 g; Carbohydrate 72 g; Fat 11 g; Cholesterol 0 mg; Sodium 1020 mg

Moroccan Garbanzo Beans with Raisins

An exotic-tasting dish that uses everyday ingredients.

1 large onion, sliced
½ cup chopped onion (about 1 medium)
1 clove garlic, finely chopped
2 tablespoons peanut oil
1 cup diced acorn or butternut squash
1 cup vegetable or chicken broth
¼ cup raisins
1 teaspoon ground turmeric
1 teaspoon ground cinnamon
½ teaspoon ground ginger
1 can (15 ounces) garbanzo beans, drained
2 cups hot cooked rice

Cook onions and garlic in oil in 3-quart saucepan about 7 minutes, stirring frequently, until tender. Stir in remaining ingredients except garbanzo beans and rice. Heat to boiling; reduce heat. Cover and simmer about 8 minutes, stirring occasionally, until squash is tender. Stir in garbanzo beans. Serve over rice.

4 servings

PER SERVING: Calories 335; Protein 8 g; Carbohydrate 66 g; Fat 5 g; Cholesterol 0 mg; Sodium 440 mg

Skillet Beans and Squash

1½ cups ¼-inch yellow squash slices (about 1½ medium)
1½ cups ¼-inch zucchini slices (about 1½ medium)
1 cup cubed peeled Hubbard or acorn squash (about 4 ounces)
½ cup chopped onion (about 1 medium)
1 cup vegetable or chicken broth
1 to 2 tablespoons chopped jalapeño chile (about 1 small)
1 large clove garlic, finely chopped
2 cans (16 ounces) kidney beans, drained
¼ cup chopped cilantro

Heat all ingredients except cilantro to boiling in 10-inch nonstick skillet; reduce heat. Cover and simmer until vegetables are tender, about 7 minutes. Stir in cilantro. **4 servings**

MICROWAVE DIRECTIONS: Decrease broth to ½ cup. Place all ingredients except beans and cilantro in 2-quart microwavable casserole. Cover tightly and microwave on high 6 minutes; stir in beans. Cover and microwave until vegetables are tender, 4 to 6 minutes longer. Stir in cilantro.

PER SERVING: Calories 100; Protein 10 g; Carbohydrate 15 g; Fat 1 g; Cholesterol 0 mg; Sodium 410 mg

Broiled Tofu

Tofu, or bean curd, takes on the flavors with which it is seasoned. Here, tofu is marinated in a savory mixture sparked with gingerroot.

¼ cup rice wine (sake) or vegetable
  broth
2 tablespoons soy sauce
2 tablespoons sesame paste
1 tablespoon sweet Japanese cooking
  wine (mirin) or vegetable broth
1 teaspoon grated gingerroot
1 pound firm tofu
Hot Mustard Sauce (below) or teriyaki
  sauce

Mix rice wine, soy sauce, sesame paste, sweet wine and gingerroot in ungreased rectanglar baking dish, 10 × 6 × ½ inch. Cut tofu into 1-inch cubes; arrange in wine mixture. Cover; refrigerate, turning tofu once, 1 hour. Soak six 8-inch bamboo or wooden skewers in water.

Thread 4 tofu cubes on each skewer. Set oven control to broil. Broil tofu with tops about 4 inches from heat until light brown, 2 to 3 minutes; turn. Brush with marinade; broil 2 to 3 minutes. Serve with Hot Mustard Sauce.

6 servings

Hot Mustard Sauce

3 tablespoons dry mustard
2 tablespoons water
1 tablespoon soy sauce

Mix all ingredients until smooth.

PER SERVING: Calories 115; Protein 8 g; Carbohydrate 5 g; Fat 7 g; Cholesterol 0 mg; Sodium 520 mg

Indian Spiced Lentils

This recipe for tender, separate (rather than soupy) lentils is a dish with character, topped with crisp-fried onions.

1 medium onion, chopped
1 clove garlic, finely chopped
2 tablespoons Ghee (page 23), margarine
  or butter
6 ounces dried red lentils (about 1 cup)
2 teaspoons ground coriander
2 teaspoons grated gingerroot
½ teaspoon salt
¼ teaspoon ground turmeric
⅛ to ¼ teaspoon ground red pepper
  (cayenne)
2½ cups water
2 tablespoons vegetable oil
2 cups finely sliced onions

Cook chopped onion and garlic in Ghee in 2-quart saucepan until tender. Stir in remaining ingredients except water, oil and sliced onions; cook and stir over medium heat 2 minutes. Add water. Heat to boiling; reduce heat. Cover and simmer until lentils are tender and most of liquid is absorbed, about 30 minutes.

Cook onion slices in oil until crisp and dark brown. Top each serving of lentils with fried onions.

4 servings

PER SERVING: Calories 330; Protein 13 g; Carbohydrate 40 g; Fat 13 g; Cholesterol 0 mg; Sodium 340 mg

Spicy Black Bean Burritos

Spicy Black Bean Burritos

By using evaporated skim milk rather than regular skim milk, you'll make a sauce that's thicker and whiter.

Pumpkin Seed Sauce (right)
1 cup chopped broccoli
½ cup chopped onion (about 1 medium)
2 cloves garlic, finely chopped
1 tablespoon reduced-calorie margarine
1 cup julienne strips yellow squash
   (about 1 medium)
2 tablespoons shelled pumpkin seeds,
   roasted
1 tablespoon lemon juice
¼ teaspoon red pepper flakes
¼ teaspoon ground cumin
1 small red bell pepper, cut into 2 × ¼-
   inch strips
1 can (15 ounces) black beans, drained
6 flour tortillas (about 8 inches in diameter), warmed

Prepare Pumpkin Seed Sauce; keep warm. Cook broccoli, onion and garlic in margarine in 10-inch nonstick skillet, stirring frequently, until onion is tender. Stir in remaining ingredients except tortillas. Cook uncovered, stirring occasionally, until squash and bell pepper are crisp-tender.

Spoon about ½ cup of the vegetable mixture onto center of each tortilla. Fold one end of tortilla up about 1 inch over mixture; fold right and left sides over, overlapping. Fold remaining end down. Serve with Pumpkin Seed Sauce.

6 servings

Pumpkin Seed Sauce

2 tablespoons chopped onion
1 small clove garlic, crushed
1 tablespoon reduced-calorie margarine
2 tablespoons shelled pumpkin seeds
1 slice whole wheat bread, torn into
   small pieces
1 tablespoon canned chopped green
   chiles
¼ cup vegetable or chicken broth
¼ cup evaporated skim milk
Dash of salt

Cook onion and garlic in margarine, stirring frequently, until onion is tender. Stir in pumpkin seeds and bread. Cook over medium heat, stirring frequently, until bread is golden brown. Stir in chiles. Place mixture in blender or food processor. Cover and blend or process until finely ground. Add broth, milk and salt. Cover and process until blended.

PER SERVING: Calories 265; Protein 13 g; Carbohydrate 37 g; Fat 8 g; Cholesterol 0 mg; Sodium 190 mg

Spicy Split Peas with Vegetables

Indian dal *is a spiced lentil, split pea, farina or dried bean mixture that is cooked almost to a smooth texture. This dish,* sambar, *takes* dal *several steps further, adding a variety of fresh vegetables. Our version of* sambar *is flavored with a sampling of the spices loved by Indians: coriander, fenugreek, cinnamon, and tamarind.*

4 cups water
1 cup dried yellow split peas
2 tablespoons shredded or flaked coconut
1 teaspoon coriander seed
½ teaspoon fenugreek seed
1 stick cinnamon, ½ inch long
1 tablespoon Ghee (page 23) or vegetable oil
¼ teaspoon salt
⅛ to ¼ teaspoon ground red pepper (cayenne)
3 medium carrots, diced
2 medium zucchini, diced
1 medium onion, finely chopped
1 small eggplant, diced
2 tablespoons Ghee (page 23) or vegetable oil
2 tablespoons water
1 tablespoon tamarind pulp
Hot cooked rice
Chopped cilantro

Heat 4 cups water and the peas to boiling in 2-quart saucepan; reduce heat. Cover and simmer 45 minutes. Cook and stir coconut, coriander, fenugreek and cinnamon in 1 tablespoon Ghee in 8-inch skillet until coconut is light brown. Remove from heat; stir in salt and red pepper. Crush coconut mixture with mortar and pestle until finely ground; reserve.

Cook carrots, zucchini, onion and eggplant in 2 tablespoons Ghee in 12-inch skillet, stirring occasionally, until tender. Stir 2 tablespoons water into tamarind pulp until softened. Stir tamarind mixture, coconut mixture and peas into skillet. Cook and stir over low heat, adding water until of consistency of soup, if necessary, until hot and well blended. Serve over rice; garnish with cilantro. **6 servings**

PER SERVING: Calories 315; Protein 11 g; Carbohydrate 52 g; Fat 7 g; Cholesterol 0 mg; Sodium 450 mg

Curried Lentils and Barley

2 teaspoons vegetable oil
½ cup chopped onion (about 1 medium)
⅓ cup coarsely chopped red or green
   bell pepper
3½ cups water
½ cup uncooked barley
1½ teaspoons curry powder
¾ teaspoon salt
1 cup thinly sliced carrots (about 2 large)
¾ cup dried lentils, sorted and rinsed
½ cup plain nonfat yogurt
¼ cup chutney

Heat oil in 3-quart saucepan over medium heat. Cook onion and bell pepper about 3 minutes, stirring occasionally, until tender. Stir in water, barley, curry powder and salt. Heat to boiling; reduce heat. Cover and simmer 15 minutes.

Stir in carrots and lentils. Heat to boiling; reduce heat. Cover and simmer 40 to 45 minutes, stirring occasionally, until lentils are tender and liquid is absorbed. Mix yogurt and chutney. Serve with lentils and barley. **4 servings**

PER SERVING: Calories 205; Protein 6 g; Carbohydrate 38 g; Fat 3 g; Cholesterol 0 mg; Sodium 470 mg

Penne with Radicchio

Radicchio is a peppery Italian chicory that is used in salads. Here it adds zest to pasta.

2 tablespoons olive oil
2 tablespoons butter
1 medium onion, thinly sliced
1 head radicchio, cut into ¼-inch strips
½ cup dry white wine or vegetable broth
1 cup whipping (heavy) cream
½ teaspoon pepper
1 package (16 ounces) penne
½ cup freshly grated Parmesan cheese

Heat oil and butter in 10-inch skillet over medium-high heat. Cook and stir onion in oil mixture. Stir in radicchio. Cover and cook over low heat 5 minutes or until tender. Stir in wine. Cook uncovered until liquid is evaporated. Stir in whipping cream and pepper. Heat to boiling; reduce heat. Simmer uncovered 30 minutes, stirring frequently, until thickened.

Cook penne as directed on package; drain. Mix penne and radicchio mixture; top with cheese. **6 servings**

PER SERVING: Calories 550; Protein 14 g; Carbohydrate 63 g; Fat 27 g; Cholesterol 70 mg; Sodium 470 mg

Vermicelli with Lemony Green Vegetables

Fettuccine with Wild Mushrooms

Dried porcini mushrooms have an intensely earthy flavor that, combined with cream, is indisputably luscious. Because the flavor is so strong, a little dried mushroom goes a long way.

1 cup hot water
1 package (about 1 ounce) dried porcini
   or cèpe mushrooms
1 small onion, chopped
2 cloves garlic, finely chopped
2 tablespoons olive or vegetable oil
1 cup whipping (heavy) cream
½ teaspoon salt
8 ounces uncooked fettuccine
Coarsely ground pepper

Pour water over mushrooms. Let stand 30 minutes; drain. Cut mushrooms into ¼-inch strips.

Cook and stir mushrooms, onion and garlic in oil in 10-inch skillet over medium heat until onion is tender. Add whipping cream and salt. Heat to boiling; reduce heat. Simmer uncovered, stirring occasionally, until slightly thickened, 3 to 5 minutes.

Cook fettuccine as directed on package; drain. Pour sauce over hot fettuccine, tossing until fettuccine is well coated. Serve with pepper.

6 servings

PER SERVING: Calories 300; Protein 6 g; Carbohydrate 28 g; Fat 18 g; Cholesterol 75 mg; Sodium 360 mg

Vermicelli with Lemony Green Vegetables

1 package (7 ounces) uncooked
   vermicelli
4 cups mixed bite-size pieces green vegetables (asparagus, broccoli, Chinese
   pea pods, green beans, zucchini)
¼ cup margarine or butter
1 tablespoon grated lemon peel
½ cup milk
1 package (3 ounces) cream cheese, cut
   into cubes and softened
½ cup grated Parmesan cheese
Salt and pepper to taste

Cook vermicelli as directed on package; drain. Cook vegetables in margarine in 10-inch skillet over medium heat, stirring frequently, until crisp-tender, about 7 minutes; toss with lemon peel. Remove vegetables; keep warm.

Heat milk and cream cheese in skillet until smooth and creamy; stir in cheese, salt and pepper. Toss with hot vermicelli. Serve vegetables over vermicelli and, if desired, with lemon wedges and coarsely ground pepper.

4 servings

PER SERVING: Calories 475; Protein 16 g; Carbohydrate 49 g; Fat 24 g; Cholesterol 35 mg; Sodium 880 mg

Savory Fusilli

Cellophane Noodles with Vegetables

Chinese cellophane noodles are, as their name implies, nearly translucent. The light strands wrap nicely around zucchini and carrots. Yellow bean paste is available in Asian groceries and specialty shops.

1 package (3¾ ounces) cellophane noodles
3 tablespoons water
1 tablespoon yellow bean paste
1 teaspoon cornstarch
1 teaspoon sugar
1 teaspoon soy sauce
2 tablespoons vegetable oil
1 medium carrot, cut into 2 × ¼-inch strips
1 clove garlic, finely chopped
1 teaspoon finely chopped gingerroot
1 medium zucchini, cut into 2 × ¼-inch strips
1 green onion, sliced

Cover noodles with hot water. Let stand 10 minutes; drain. Cut into 2-inch lengths. Mix 3 tablespoons water, the bean paste, cornstarch, sugar and soy sauce; reserve.

Heat oil in wok or 10-inch skillet until hot. Add carrot, garlic and gingerroot. Stir-fry 1 minute. Add zucchini; stir-fry 2 minutes. Add noodles and bean paste mixture; stir-fry 45 seconds. Sprinkle with green onion. **4 servings**

PER SERVING: Calories 145; Protein 1 g; Carbohydrate 20 g; Fat 7 g; Cholesterol 0 mg; Sodium 360 mg

Savory Fusilli

This dish is also very nice chilled and served as a salad.

¼ cup olive oil
1 tablespoon capers, drained
3 cloves garlic, finely chopped
2 cans (28 ounces each) imported pear-shaped tomatoes, drained and chopped
1 small red chile, seeded and chopped
½ cup sliced imported Italian black olives
½ cup sliced green olives
1 tablespoon chopped fresh oregano leaves
1 tablespoon chopped fresh basil leaves
1 package (16 ounces) fusilli (spiral pasta)
Coarsely ground pepper

Heat oil in 10-inch skillet over medium-high heat. Sauté capers and garlic in oil. Stir in tomatoes and chile. Heat to boiling; reduce heat. Cover and simmer 20 minutes, stirring occasionally. Stir in olives, oregano and basil. Cover and cook 10 minutes.

Cook fusilli as directed on package; drain. Mix fusilli and tomato mixture. Serve with pepper. **6 servings**

PER SERVING: Calories 470; Protein 13 g; Carbohydrate 73 g; Fat 14 g; Cholesterol 0 mg; Sodium 1100 mg

Rotini with Fresh Herbs

A wonderful pasta to make in summer, or any time when you have access to fresh herbs.

2 tablespoons chopped fresh mint leaves
2 tablespoons chopped parsley
2 tablespoons chopped fresh basil leaves
2 tablespoons chopped fresh dill weed
1 pound fresh spinach*
½ cup water
2 tablespoons butter
2 cloves garlic, finely chopped
1 cup whipping (heavy) cream
½ teaspoon salt
½ teaspoon pepper
1 package (16 ounces) vegetable-flavored rotini
½ cup freshly grated Parmesan cheese

Mix mint, parsley, basil and dill weed; cover with cold water. Let stand 1 hour; drain and pat dry.

Heat spinach and water to boiling. Cover and cook about 5 minutes or until tender; drain well. Heat butter in 10-inch skillet over medium-high heat. Sauté garlic in butter. Stir in herbs, spinach, whipping cream, salt and pepper. Heat to boiling; reduce heat. Cover and simmer 20 minutes, stirring frequently.

Cook rotini as directed on package; drain. Mix rotini and sauce; top with cheese. Garnish with fresh herb leaves if desired. **6 servings**

*1 package (10 ounces) frozen chopped spinach can be substituted for the fresh spinach. Cook as directed on package; drain well.

PER SERVING: Calories 500; Protein 15 g; Carbohydrate 56 g; Fat 24 g; Cholesterol 140 mg; Sodium 730 mg

Three-Cheese Tortellini

1 package (7 ounces) dried cheese-filled tortellini
¼ cup margarine or butter
½ cup chopped green bell pepper
2 shallots, finely chopped
1 clove garlic, finely chopped
¼ cup all-purpose flour
¼ teaspoon pepper
1¾ cups milk
½ cup shredded mozzarella cheese (2 ounces)
½ cup shredded Swiss cheese (2 ounces)
¼ cup grated Parmesan or Romano cheese

Cook tortellini as directed on package; drain. Heat margarine in 3-quart saucepan over medium heat. Cook bell pepper, shallots and garlic in margarine about 3 minutes. Stir in flour and pepper. Cook, stirring constantly, until mixture is bubbly; remove from heat. Stir in milk. Heat to boiling, stirring constantly. Boil and stir 1 minute; remove from heat. Stir in mozzarella and Swiss cheeses until melted. Add tortellini and stir until coated. Sprinkle with Parmesan cheese.

5 servings

PER SERVING: Calories 390; Protein 16 g; Carbohydrate 41 g; Fat 18 g; Cholesterol 30 mg; Sodium 300 mg

Welsh Rabbit

This cheese treat doesn't contain rabbit, but does have lots of great taste!

3 tablespoons margarine or butter
3 tablespoons all-purpose flour
¼ teaspoon salt
¼ teaspoon pepper
¼ teaspoon dry mustard
¼ teaspoon Worcestershire sauce
1 cup milk
½ cup beer or white wine*
1½ cups shredded Cheddar cheese
  (6 ounces)
4 slices toast, cut into triangles

Heat margarine in 2-quart saucepan over medium heat until melted. Stir in flour, salt, pepper, mustard and Worcestershire sauce. Cook, stirring constantly, until smooth and bubbly; remove from heat. Stir in milk. Heat to boiling, stirring constantly. Boil and stir 1 minute. Gradually stir in beer. Stir in cheese. Heat over low heat, stirring constantly, until cheese is melted. Serve over toast. Sprinkle with paprika if desired.

4 servings

Beer or wine can be omitted. Increase milk to 1½ cups.

ASPARAGUS WELSH RABBIT: Cook 1 package (10 ounces) frozen asparagus spears as directed on package; drain. Arrange on toast before topping with cheese sauce.

PER SERVING: Calories 390; Protein 16 g; Carbohydrate 23 g; Fat 25 g; Cholesterol 50 mg; Sodium 680 mg

Cheese Tips

- To shred a small amount of cheese, pull a swivel-bladed vegetable parer over the edge of firm cheese.

- Freeze cheese in small amounts in tightly wrapped packages up to 4 months. Thaw cheese in refrigerator to prevent crumbling.

- Save leftover cheese bits to blend with cream for spreads and dips.

- Very soft cheese shreds more easily if first placed in the freezer for fifteen minutes. Or it can be finely chopped instead of shredded.

Macaroni Ring with Creamed Peas (page 56)

3

Creative Casseroles

Cheese Manicotti

1 package (8 ounces) manicotti shells
10 ounces fresh spinach
1½ cups small curd creamed cottage cheese
¼ cup grated Parmesan cheese
1 tablespoon vegetable or chicken bouillon granules
¾ teaspoon chopped fresh or ⅛ teaspoon dried thyme leaves
2 eggs
1 small onion, chopped (about ¼ cup)
1 clove garlic, crushed
1 can (8 ounces) tomato sauce
1 cup shredded mozzarella cheese (4 ounces)

Heat oven to 350°. Grease rectangular baking dish, 13 × 9 × 2 inches. Cook manicotti shells as directed on package; drain.

Wash spinach; drain and chop. Cover and cook with just the water that clings to the leaves about 3 minutes or until tender; drain.

Mix remaining ingredients except tomato sauce and mozzarella cheese. Fill manicotti shells with spinach mixture. Place in baking dish. Pour tomato sauce over shells. Sprinkle with mozzarella cheese. Cover and bake about 25 minutes or until hot. **5 servings**

PER SERVING: Calories 390; Protein 25 g; Carbohydrate 43 g; Fat 13 g; Cholesterol 160 mg; Sodium 1060 mg

Macaroni Ring with Creamed Peas

**2 cups uncooked elbow macaroni
(8 ounces)
2 cups hot milk
2 cups shredded Cheddar cheese
(8 ounces)
2 cups soft bread crumbs
¼ cup margarine or butter
2 tablespoons chopped parsley
2 tablespoons finely chopped onion
2 tablespoons chopped pimiento
½ teaspoon salt
¼ teaspoon pepper
2 eggs, slightly beaten
Creamed Peas (below)**

Cook macaroni as directed on package; drain. Heat oven to 350°. Grease 10-inch ring mold. Mix macaroni and remaining ingredients except Creamed Peas. Pour into mold; place in pan of very hot water (1 inch deep). Bake 35 to 40 minutes or until set. Remove mold from water; let stand 5 minutes. Loosen sides with metal spatula. Unmold ring on large platter; fill center with Creamed Peas.   **8 servings**

Creamed Peas

**2 pounds fresh green peas*
2 tablespoons finely chopped onion
2 tablespoons margarine or butter
2 tablespoons all-purpose flour
¼ teaspoon salt
1½ cups milk**

Heat 1 inch salted water (¼ teaspoon salt, if desired, to 1 cup water) to boiling; add peas. Heat to boiling; reduce heat. Cook uncovered 5 minutes. Cover and cook 3 to 7 minutes or until tender; drain.

Cook and stir onion in margarine in 2-quart saucepan until tender. Stir in flour and salt. Cook over low heat, stirring constantly, until mixture is bubbly; remove from heat. Stir in milk. Heat to boiling, stirring constantly. Boil and stir 1 minute. Stir in peas gently; heat through.

*1 package (10 ounces) frozen green peas, cooked and drained, or 1 can (16 ounces) green peas, drained, can be substituted for the fresh green peas.

PER SERVING: Calories 570; Protein 25 g; Carbohydrate 66 g; Fat 23 g; Cholesterol 115 mg; Sodium 900 mg

Vegetable Lasagne

A dish that's easy to assemble, then you can relax while it cooks.

**3 cups chunky-style spaghetti sauce
1 medium zucchini, shredded
6 uncooked lasagne noodles
1 cup ricotta or small curd creamed
cottage cheese
¼ cup grated Parmesan cheese
3 teaspoons chopped fresh or 1 teaspoon dried oregano leaves
2 cups shredded mozzarella cheese
(8 ounces)**

Heat oven to 350°. Mix spaghetti sauce and zucchini. Spread 1 cup of the sauce mixture in ungreased rectangular baking dish, 11 × 7 × 1½ inches. Top with 3 noodles. Mix ricotta cheese, Parmesan cheese and oregano; spread over noodles in dish. Spread with 1 cup of the sauce mixture.

Top with remaining noodles, sauce mixture and the mozzarella cheese. Bake uncovered about 45 minutes or until hot and bubbly. Let stand 15 minutes before cutting.   **8 servings**

PER SERVING: Calories 275; Protein 15 g; Carbohydrate 22 g; Fat 14 g; Cholesterol 45 mg; Sodium 190 mg

Macaroni con Queso

A southwest twist on an old favorite.

Chile con Queso (below)
4 ounces uncooked elbow macaroni or
macaroni shells (about 1 cup)
1 large tomato, chopped (about 1 cup)
1 tablespoon chopped cilantro
1 cup shredded Cheddar or Monterey
Jack cheese (4 ounces)
¼ cup crushed tortilla chips

Heat oven to 375°. Prepare Chile con Queso; reserve. Cook macaroni as directed on package; drain.

Mix macaroni, Chile con Queso, tomato and cilantro in ungreased 1½-quart casserole. Sprinkle with cheese and tortilla chips. Bake uncovered until hot, about 30 minutes.

4 servings

Chile con Queso

1 cup shredded Cheddar or Monterey
Jack cheese (4 ounces)
½ cup milk
¼ cup half-and-half
2 tablespoons finely chopped onion
2 teaspoons ground cumin
½ teaspoon salt
1 can (4 ounces) chopped green chiles,
drained

Heat all ingredients over low heat, stirring constantly, until cheese is melted.

PER SERVING: Calories 420; Protein 21 g; Carbohydrate 34 g; Fat 22 g; Cholesterol 70 mg; Sodium 1030 mg

Cheese Enchiladas

2 cups shredded Monterey Jack cheese
(8 ounces)
1 cup shredded Cheddar cheese
(4 ounces)
1 medium onion, chopped (about ½ cup)
½ cup sour cream or plain yogurt
2 tablespoons chopped fresh parsley
¼ teaspoon pepper
6 flour tortillas (7-inch diameter)
⅓ cup chopped green bell pepper
1 tablespoon chile powder
1 teaspoon chopped fresh or ½ teaspoon
dried oregano leaves
¼ teaspoon ground cumin
1 clove garlic, finely chopped
1 can (15 ounces) tomato sauce
¼ cup shredded Cheddar cheese
(1 ounce)

Heat oven to 350°. Grease rectangular baking dish, 12 × 7½ × 2 inches. Mix Monterey Jack cheese, 1 cup Cheddar cheese, the onion, sour cream, parsley and pepper. Spoon about ½ cup cheese mixture onto each tortilla. Roll tortilla around filling and place seam side down in dish. Mix remaining ingredients except ¼ cup Cheddar cheese. Pour over enchiladas. Sprinkle with ¼ cup Cheddar cheese. Bake uncovered about 20 minutes or until hot and bubbly. Garnish with sour cream and sliced black olives or lime wedges if desired. **6 servings**

TO MICROWAVE: Prepare as directed—except place enchiladas in greased rectangular microwavable dish, 12 × 7½ × 2 inches, and do not sprinkle with ¼ cup Cheddar cheese. Cover with waxed paper and microwave on high 9 to 11 minutes, rotating dish ½ turn after 5 minutes, until hot and bubbly. Sprinkle with ¼ cup Cheddar cheese. Cover and let stand about 3 minutes.

PER SERVING: Calories 360; Protein 18 g; Carbohydrate 19 g; Fat 24 g; Cholesterol 35 mg; Sodium 780 mg

Enchiladas with Green Sauce

These Mexican enchiladas *are gently seasoned with mild green chiles. The classic recipe for green sauce is based on* tomatillos, *vegetables that look like bright, acid green tomatoes in miniature. Spinach, more widely available in the United States, is used here.*

Cheese Filling (below)
Green Sauce (right)
Eight 6-inch tortillas

Prepare Cheese Filling and Green Sauce. Heat tortillas, one at a time, in ungreased hot skillet until softened, about 30 seconds. (Cover hot tortillas to prevent drying.) Dip each tortilla into Green Sauce to coat both sides. Spoon about ¼ cup Cheese Filling onto each tortilla; roll tortilla around filling to form enchilada.

Arrange enchiladas, seam sides down, in ungreased rectangular baking dish, 12 × 7½ × 2 inches. Pour remaining sauce over enchiladas. Cook uncovered in 350° oven until bubbly, about 20 minutes. Garnish with shredded Cheddar or Monterey Jack cheese and lime wedges if desired. **4 servings**

Cheese Filling

2 cups shredded Monterey Jack cheese (8 ounces)
1 cup shredded Cheddar cheese (4 ounces)
½ cup sour cream
2 tablespoons chopped parsley
1 teaspoon salt
¼ teaspoon pepper
1 medium onion, chopped

Mix all ingredients.

Green Sauce

10 ounces fresh spinach (about 6 cups)*
2 tablespoons margarine or butter
2 tablespoons all-purpose flour
¼ teaspoon salt
½ cup milk
1½ cups vegetable or chicken broth
1 to 2 tablespoons chopped canned green chiles
⅔ cup sour cream
¾ teaspoon ground cumin
1 small onion, chopped
1 clove garlic, finely chopped

Wash spinach; cover and cook with just the water that clings to leaves until tender, 3 to 5 minutes. Drain and pat dry; chop coarsely.

Heat margarine over low heat until melted. Blend in flour and salt. Cook over low heat, stirring constantly, until smooth and bubbly; remove from heat. Stir in milk and ½ cup of the broth; heat to boiling, stirring constantly. Boil and stir 1 minute. Stir in remaining broth. Cook and stir over low heat until hot; remove from heat. Stir in spinach and remaining ingredients.

*1 package (10 ounces) frozen chopped spinach, cooked and well drained, can be substituted for the fresh spinach.

PER SERVING: Calories 775; Protein 34 g; Carbohydrate 47 g; Fat 50 g; Cholesterol 135 mg; Sodium 1980 mg

Ricotta Cheese Enchiladas

These enchiladas are a southwestern version of manicotti. The cilantro and nut sauce are nice counterpoints to the rich ricotta filling.

Roasted Tomato Sauce (right)
1 container (15 ounces) ricotta cheese
1 cup shredded Monterey Jack cheese
(4 ounces)
¼ cup grated Sierra or Romano cheese
(1 ounce)
2 tablespoons chopped cilantro
1 small onion, finely chopped (about ¼
cup)
2 eggs
10 flour tortillas (8 inches in diameter),
warmed
½ cup shredded Monterey Jack cheese
(2 ounces)
Cilantro Pesto (right)

Prepare Roasted Tomato Sauce; reserve. Heat oven to 350°. Mix ricotta cheese, 1 cup Monterey Jack cheese, the Sierra cheese, cilantro, onion and eggs. Spoon about ⅓ cup mixture onto each tortilla; roll up. Place seam sides down in greased rectangular pan, 13 × 9 × 2 inches. Pour Roasted Tomato Sauce over top.

Bake uncovered until filling is set, about 40 minutes. Sprinkle with ½ cup Monterey Jack cheese; bake until cheese is melted, 3 to 4 minutes. Serve with Cilantro Pesto.

5 servings

Roasted Tomato Sauce

2 pounds tomatoes, cored
1 medium onion, chopped (about ½ cup)
¼ cup finely chopped carrot
1 tablespoon vegetable oil
1 tablespoon chopped fresh basil leaves
2 teaspoons sugar
1 teaspoon chopped fresh oregano
leaves
¼ teaspoon salt
¼ teaspoon ground red pepper (cayenne)

Set oven control to broil. Arrange tomatoes with their top surfaces about 5 inches from the heat. Broil, turning occasionally, until the skin is blistered and evenly browned, 5 to 8 minutes. The skins will be easy to remove.

Cook onion and carrot in oil over medium heat, stirring occasionally, until tender. Cut tomatoes into fourths; drain.

Place onion, carrot, tomatoes and remaining ingredients in blender or food processor. Cover and blend or process until well mixed.

Cilantro Pesto

1½ cups firmly packed cilantro
½ cup firmly packed parsley
½ cup grated Parmesan cheese
½ cup vegetable oil
¼ teaspoon salt
3 cloves garlic
¼ cup pine nuts (1 ounce)

Place all ingredients in blender or food processor. Cover and blend or process until mixed.

PER SERVING: Calories 940; Protein 35 g; Carbohydrate 69 g; Fat 58 g; Cholesterol 160 mg; Sodium 1140 mg

Refried-Bean Roll-ups

8 flour tortillas (7 to 8 inches in
   diameter)
1 can (16 ounces) refried beans
½ cup salsa
½ teaspoon chile powder
1 cup shredded lettuce
½ cup shredded Monterey Jack cheese
   (2 ounces)

Heat oven to 250°. Wrap tortillas in aluminum foil or place on heatproof serving plate and cover with aluminum foil. Heat about 15 minutes or until warm.

Mix beans, salsa and chile powder in saucepan. Heat over medium heat 5 minutes, stirring occasionally, until warm. Place about ¼ cup mixture in center of each tortilla; spread slightly. Top with about 2 tablespoons lettuce and 1 tablespoon cheese. Fold over sides and ends. Serve with extra salsa if desired. **4 servings**

PER SERVING: Calories 460; Protein 17 g; Carbohydrate 71 g; Fat 12 g; Cholesterol 20 mg; Sodium 1210 mg

Italian-style Baked Beans

4 cups water
1 pound dried lima or great northern
   beans (about 2 cups)
1½ teaspoons salt
2 tablespoons margarine or butter
¾ cup chopped onion
¾ cup chopped green bell pepper
1 clove garlic, finely chopped
½ cup sliced pitted ripe olives
¼ cup grated Parmesan cheese
2 to 3 teaspoons chile powder
1 can (6 ounces) tomato paste

Heat water and beans to boiling in Dutch oven. Boil 2 minutes; remove from heat. Cover and let stand 1 hour.

Add enough water to beans to cover if necessary. Stir in salt. Heat to boiling; reduce heat. Cover and simmer 45 to 60 minutes or until tender (do not boil or beans will burst).

Heat oven to 375°. Drain beans; reserve liquid. Add enough water to the bean liquid, if necessary, to measure 1 cup. Heat margarine in 10-inch skillet until melted. Stir in onion, bell pepper and garlic. Cook, stirring frequently, until onion is tender. Stir in beans, reserved bean liquid and remaining ingredients. Pour into ungreased 2-quart casserole. Bake uncovered about 30 minutes or until hot and bubbly. **6 servings**

PER SERVING: Calories 375; Protein 19 g; Carbohydrate 58 g; Fat 9 g; Cholesterol 5 mg; Sodium 980 mg

Bean-Stuffed Cabbage Rolls

For variety, try different types of beans, such as pinto, kidney or black beans.

1 large head cabbage (about 3 pounds)
1 tablespoon reduced-calorie margarine
¼ cup chopped onion (about 1 small)
2 teaspoons chopped fresh or ½ teaspoon dried sage leaves
¼ teaspoon ground cumin
1 clove garlic, finely chopped
1½ cups finely shredded cabbage
½ cup shredded carrot (about 1 medium)
1 can (19 ounces) cannellini beans, drained
½ cup vegetable or chicken broth
½ cup skim milk
2 teaspoons cornstarch
1 teaspoon chopped fresh or ¼ teaspoon dried sage leaves
¼ teaspoon salt
6 tablespoons shredded low-fat Swiss cheese

Remove core from cabbage. Cover cabbage with warm water; let stand about 10 minutes or until leaves loosen slightly. Remove 12 cabbage leaves. Cover leaves with boiling water. Cover and let stand about 10 minutes or until leaves are limp; drain.

Heat oven to 350°. Heat margarine in 2-quart nonstick saucepan over medium heat. Cook onion, 2 teaspoons chopped fresh sage, the cumin and garlic about 3 minutes, stirring frequently, until onion is softened. Stir in shredded cabbage, carrot and beans.

Place scant ¼ cup bean mixture at stem end of cabbage leaf. Roll leaf around bean mixture, tucking in sides. Place cabbage rolls, seam sides down, in ungreased rectangular baking dish, 13 × 9 × 2 inches. Pour broth over rolls.

Cover and bake 30 to 35 minutes or until rolls are hot.

Remove cabbage rolls with slotted spoon; keep warm. Drain liquid from baking dish, reserving ½ cup. Gradually stir milk into cornstarch in saucepan until smooth; stir in reserved liquid, 1 teaspoon chopped fresh sage and the salt. Heat to boiling over medium heat, stirring constantly. Boil and stir 1 minute. Serve sauce over cabbage rolls; sprinkle each serving with 1 tablespoon cheese. **6 servings**

PER SERVING: Calories 175; Protein 8 g; Carbohydrate 32 g; Fat 3 g; Cholesterol 0 mg; Sodium 450 mg

Designer Casseroles

Add your own touch of creativity to your casseroles by using a simple topping or garnish. Use the list below to add flavor, color or texture to your favorite casseroles after they have been baked.

Shredded or grated cheese such as: Cheddar, Monterey Jack, mozzarella, Parmesan or Romano

Sliced bell pepper strips

Pimiento strips

Jalapeño slices

Sliced ripe, green or stuffed green olives

Tomato wedges

Sliced hard-cooked eggs

Chopped fresh herbs such as: chervil, chives, cilantro or parsley

Crushed potato, tortilla or corn chips

Bean-Cheese Pie

Bean-Cheese Pie

¾ cup all-purpose flour
½ cup shredded Cheddar cheese
  (2 ounces)
1½ teaspoons baking powder
½ teaspoon salt
⅓ cup milk
1 egg, slightly beaten
½ cup chopped green bell pepper (about
  1 small)
¼ cup chopped onion (about 1 small)
2 teaspoons chile powder
2 teaspoons fresh or ½ teaspoon dried
  oregano leaves
¼ teaspoon garlic powder
1 can (15½ ounces) garbanzo beans,
  drained
1 can (15 ounces) kidney beans, drained
1 can (8 ounces) tomato sauce
½ cup shredded Cheddar cheese
  (2 ounces)

Heat oven to 375°. Spray pie plate, 10 × 1½ inches, with nonstick cooking spray. Mix flour, ½ cup cheese, the baking powder and salt in medium bowl. Stir in milk and egg until blended. Spread over bottom and up side of pie plate. Mix remaining ingredients except ½ cup cheese. Spoon into pie plate; sprinkle with ½ cup cheese. Bake uncovered about 25 minutes or until edge is puffy and light brown. Let stand 10 minutes before cutting. **8 servings**

PER SERVING: Calories 315; Protein 18 g; Carbohydrate 40 g; Fat 11 g; Cholesterol 50 mg; Sodium 730 mg

Rice and Cheese Casserole

2 cups water
1 cup uncooked regular long grain rice
½ teaspoon salt
½ teaspoon dry mustard
¼ teaspoon pepper
⅛ to ¼ teaspoon red pepper sauce
1 medium onion, chopped (about ½ cup)
1 medium green bell pepper, chopped
  (about 1 cup)
2 eggs
2 egg whites
2 cups milk
1 cup shredded mozzarella cheese
  (4 ounces)
2 tablespoons grated Parmesan cheese

Heat water, rice, salt, mustard, pepper and the pepper sauce to boiling in 1½-quart saucepan, stirring once or twice; reduce heat. Cover and simmer 14 minutes. (Do not lift cover or stir.) Remove from heat. Fluff lightly with fork. Cover and let steam 5 to 10 minutes. Stir in onion and bell pepper.

Heat oven to 325°. Grease rectangular baking dish, 11 × 7 × 1½ inches. Pour rice mixture into baking dish. Mix eggs, egg whites and milk; pour over rice mixture. Sprinkle with cheeses. Bake uncovered 40 to 45 minutes or until golden brown and set. Let stand 10 minutes before serving. **4 servings**

PER SERVING: Calories 220; Protein 16 g; Carbohydrate 12 g; Fat 12 g; Cholesterol 140 mg; Sodium 550 mg

Bulgur-Walnut Casserole

This hearty casserole is full of crunch as well as protein, thanks to the addition of walnuts.

1½ cups uncooked bulgur
1½ cups cold water
1½ cups coarsely chopped walnuts
¼ cup chopped parsley
1 teaspoon dried basil leaves
½ teaspoon salt
¼ teaspoon ground coriander
⅛ teaspoon pepper
1 medium onion, chopped (about ½ cup)
1 small green bell pepper, chopped (about ½ cup)
2 eggs, slightly beaten
1 can (8 ounces) tomato sauce
1 jar (2 ounces) diced pimientos, drained
Cheese Sauce (below)

Cover bulgur with water. Let stand 1 hour.

Heat oven to 350°. Mix bulgur and remaining ingredients except Cheese Sauce. Spread mixture in ungreased 1½-quart casserole. Bake uncovered about 35 minutes or until light brown. Serve with Cheese Sauce.   **5 servings**

Cheese Sauce

2 tablespoons margarine or butter
2 tablespoons all-purpose flour
¼ teaspoon salt
Dash of ground red pepper (cayenne)
1 cup milk
1 cup shredded Cheddar cheese (4 ounces)

Heat margarine in 1-quart saucepan over low heat until melted. Stir in flour, salt and red pepper until blended. Cook over low heat, stirring constantly, until smooth and bubbly; remove from heat. Stir in milk. Heat to boiling, stirring constantly. Boil and stir 1 minute. Stir in cheese until melted.

PER SERVING; Calories 605; Protein 21 g; Carbohydrate 57 g; Fat 35 g; Cholesterol 115 mg; Sodium 830 mg

Chilaquiles Casserole

4 flour tortillas (about 8 inches in diameter), cut into ½-inch strips
1 can (16 ounces) pinto beans, drained
1 bottle (16 ounces) red or green salsa (about 1¾ cups)
2 cups shredded Monterey Jack cheese (8 ounces)
⅓ cup low-fat sour cream
⅓ cup plain nonfat yogurt
1 tablespoon chopped cilantro or parsley

Heat oven to 350°. Spray 2-quart casserole with nonstick cooking spray. Layer half of the tortilla strips in bottom of casserole. Top with beans, half of the salsa and 1 cup of the cheese. Repeat with remaining tortilla strips, salsa and cheese. Bake uncovered about 30 minutes or until cheese is melted and golden brown.

Mix sour cream, yogurt and cilantro. Top each serving with about 2 tablespoons sour cream mixture.   **6 servings**

PER SERVING: Calories 295; Protein 15 g; Carbohydrate 26 g; Fat 15 g; Cholesterol 45 mg; Sodium 1070 mg

Chile–Tofu Casserole

1 can (8 ounces) tomato sauce
1 medium onion, chopped (about ½ cup)
1 large clove garlic, crushed
½ teaspoon salt
½ teaspoon dried oregano leaves
¼ teaspoon ground cumin
2 pounds firm tofu, cut into ½-inch slices
1 can (4 ounces) chopped green chiles, drained
1 cup shredded Cheddar cheese (4 ounces)

Heat oven to 350°. Grease square baking dish, 8 × 8 × 2 inches. Mix tomato sauce, onion, garlic, salt, oregano and cumin. Spread half of the tomato mixture in baking dish. Arrange tofu on tomato sauce, overlapping slices. Sprinkle with chiles. Spread with remaining tomato mixture. Sprinkle with cheese. Bake uncovered about 15 minutes or until sauce is hot.   **6 servings**

PER SERVING: Calories 320; Protein 29 g; Carbohydrate 13 g; Fat 20 g; Cholesterol 20 mg; Sodium 530 mg

The Second Time Around

Nutritious and quick to heat in the microwave, enjoy casseroles for breakfasts, lunches or snacks. To zap your leftover casserole quickly in the microwave, remember to cover it and stir it once or twice while microwaving.

If your casserole can't be stirred, allow it to stand covered after microwaving to finish heating throughout.

To help prevent overcooking, use a lower power setting on casseroles that contain delicate foods such as eggs and cheese.

Cheese Soufflé

Years ago, American restaurants touted the cheese soufflé as the epitome of French cuisine. Many soufflés are in fact simple dishes, easy to prepare and requiring little as an accompaniment. This cheese soufflé would be delicious served with a lightly dressed lettuce salad and some good, crusty bread.

¼ cup margarine or butter
¼ cup all-purpose flour
½ teaspoon salt
Dash of ground red pepper (cayenne)
1 cup milk
1 cup shredded Swiss or Gruyère cheese (4 ounces)
4 eggs, separated
¼ teaspoon cream of tartar

Heat margarine in 2-quart saucepan over low heat until melted. Blend in flour, salt and red pepper. Cook over low heat, stirring constantly, until mixture is smooth and bubbly; remove from heat. Stir in milk. Heat to boiling, stirring constantly. Boil and stir 1 minute. Stir in cheese until melted; remove from heat.

Heat oven to 325°. Beat egg whites and cream of tartar in large bowl on high speed until stiff but not dry. Beat egg yolks in small mixer bowl until very thick and lemon-colored, about 5 minutes; stir into cheese mixture. Stir about one-quarter of the egg whites into cheese mixture. Fold cheese mixture into remaining egg whites.

Carefully pour into greased 1½-quart soufflé dish or casserole. Cook uncovered in oven until knife inserted halfway between center and edge comes out clean, 50 to 60 minutes. Serve immediately.   **4 servings**

PER SERVING: Calories 335; Protein 17 g; Carbohydrate 11 g; Fat 25 g; Cholesterol 240 mg; Sodium 580 mg

Winter Squash Soufflé

Winter Squash Soufflé

¼ cup chopped onion (about 1 small)
2 tablespoons reduced-calorie margarine
2 tablespoons all-purpose flour
¼ teaspoon salt
¼ teaspoon ground nutmeg
⅛ teaspoon pepper
1 cup skim milk
3 eggs, separated
1 package (12 ounces) frozen squash, thawed
2 egg whites
½ teaspoon cream of tartar
2 teaspoons grated Parmesan cheese

Heat oven to 350°. Make a 4-inch band of triple-thickness aluminum foil 2 inches longer than circumference of 6-cup soufflé dish or 1½-quart casserole; secure foil band around top edge of dish. Spray inside of dish and foil with nonstick cooking spray.

Cook onion in margarine in 2-quart nonstick saucepan until onion is softened. Stir in flour, salt, nutmeg and pepper. Cook over low heat, stirring constantly, until margarine is absorbed; remove from heat. Beat milk and egg yolks; stir into flour mixture. Heat to boiling, stirring constantly. Boil and stir 1 minute. Stir in squash.

Beat egg whites and cream of tartar in medium bowl on high speed until stiff but not dry. Stir about one-quarter of the egg white mixture into squash mixture. Fold squash mixture into remaining egg white mixture.

Carefully pour into soufflé dish. Bake uncovered about 50 minutes or until set and cracks feel dry when touched lightly. Carefully remove foil band and divide soufflé into 4 servings with 2 forks. Sprinkle each serving with Parmesan cheese. Serve immediately. **4 servings**

PER SERVING: Calories 195; Protein 11 g; Carbohydrate 17 g; Fat 9 g; Cholesterol 165 mg; Sodium 330 mg

Quick Chile-Cheese Puff

We've kept calories low and taste high in this no-fuss main dish.

1 cup shredded sharp Cheddar cheese (4 ounces)
2 cans (4 ounces each) whole green chiles, drained
¼ cup all-purpose flour
½ cup skim milk
¼ teaspoon pepper
2 eggs

Heat oven to 350°. Layer half of the cheese, the chiles and remaining cheese in 1-quart casserole or four 10-ounce custard cups sprayed with nonstick cooking spray. Beat remaining ingredients with rotary beater until smooth; pour over top. Bake until puffy and golden brown, casserole about 40 minutes, custard cups about 20 minutes. **4 servings**

PER SERVING: Calories 200; Protein 12 g; Carbohydrate 10 g; Fat 12 g; Cholesterol 170 mg; Sodium 240 mg

Egg Smarts

- What's your Egg I.Q.? Brown eggs versus white—which have more food value? Actually, there is no difference; shell color is determined by the breed of hen that lays the egg.

- Look for eggs in shells that are clean and whole. If a shell cracks between the market and home, use it as soon as possible in a fully cooked dish.

- There is very little difference in quality between Grades AA and A, and there is no difference in nutritive content.

- Egg sizes are based on the weight per dozen: Jumbo (30 ounces), Extra Large (24 ounces), Medium (21 ounces) and Small (18 ounces).

Mushroom-Cheese Soufflé

Extra egg whites account for the extra large serving size of this delicious soufflé.

3 cups finely chopped mushrooms (about 12 ounces)
2 tablespoons finely chopped onion
1 large clove garlic, finely chopped
3 tablespoons reduced-calorie margarine
2 tablespoons all-purpose flour
⅛ teaspoon ground red pepper (cayenne)
1 cup skim milk
2 egg yolks
⅓ cup grated Parmesan cheese
5 egg whites
½ teaspoon cream of tartar

Heat oven to 350°. Spray 6-cup soufflé dish or 1½-quart casserole with nonstick cooking spray. Make a 4-inch band of triple-thickness aluminum foil 2 inches longer than circumference of dish; spray 1 side with nonstick cooking spray. Secure foil band, sprayed side in, around top edge of dish.

Cook mushrooms, onion and garlic in 1 tablespoon of the margarine in 10-inch nonstick skillet until all the moisture is evaporated, about 5 minutes; drain well.

Heat remaining 2 tablespoons margarine in 1½-quart saucepan over low heat until melted. Stir in flour and red pepper. Cook over low heat, stirring constantly, until smooth and bubbly, about 30 seconds. Remove from heat. Beat milk and egg yolks; stir into flour mixture. Heat to boiling, stirring constantly. Boil and stir 1 minute. Stir in cheese; remove from heat. Stir in mushroom mixture.

Beat egg whites and cream of tartar in medium bowl on high speed until stiff but not dry. Stir about one-quarter of the egg white mixture into mushroom mixture. Fold mushroom mixture into remaining egg white mixture.

Carefully pour into soufflé dish. Bake uncovered until golden brown and cracks feel dry when touched lightly, about 45 minutes. Carefully remove foil band and divide soufflé into 4 sections with 2 forks. Serve immediately.

4 servings

PER SERVING: Calories 200; Protein 12 g; Carbohydrate 11 g; Fat 12 g; Cholesterol 140 mg; Sodium 320 mg

Double Cheese and Potato Casserole

2 cups shredded Cheddar cheese (8 ounces)
5 eggs
1 cup small curd creamed cottage cheese
1½ cups water
1 cup milk
1 teaspoon dry mustard
½ teaspoon salt
¼ teaspoon red pepper sauce
1 bunch green onions, sliced
1 package (6 ounces) hash brown potatoes (dry)

Heat oven to 350°. Reserve 1 cup of the Cheddar cheese. Beat eggs in ungreased rectangular baking dish, 12 × 7½ × 2 inches; beat in remaining ingredients. Sprinkle with reserved Cheddar cheese.

Bake uncovered until knife inserted in center comes out clean, 40 to 45 minutes.

6 servings

PER SERVING: Calories; 335; Protein 21 g; Carbohydrate 11 g; Fat 23 g; Cholesterol 230 mg; Sodium 710 mg

Alpine Cheese Supper

This dish, also known as raclette, is simple: cheese, pickles, potatoes and onions. The traditional Swiss way with raclette is to place the wheel of cheese on the hearth, close enough to the fire so that the cheese begins to melt. Raclette is scraped (racler means "to scrape," in French) from the wheel as it melts and is served with the vegetables.

2 pounds new potatoes (12 to 14)
1 pound imported Swiss raclette cheese*
Fresh ground pepper
1 jar (8 ounces) midget dill pickles or gherkins
1 jar (8 ounces) pickled cocktail onions

Heat 1 inch salted water (1 teaspoon salt to 1 cup water) to boiling. Add potatoes. Heat to boiling; reduce heat. Cover and cook until tender, 20 to 25 minutes; drain. Keep warm.

Cut cheese into 4 pieces; divide among 4 individual ovenproof casseroles. Heat in 400° oven until cheese is melted, about 10 minutes.

Place each hot casserole on a dinner plate. Sprinkle potatoes with pepper, then swirl in melted cheese. Eat the potatoes alternately with pickles and onions.   **4 servings**

*Other cheeses that melt smoothly and easily, such as Gruyère, Muenster, Fontina, Swiss or Monterey Jack, can be substituted for the raclette cheese.

PER SERVING: Calories 670; Protein 37 g; Carbohydrate 61 g; Fat 31 g; Cholesterol 105 mg; Sodium 920 mg

Spiced Cottage Cheese with Greens

Seasoned cheese and collard greens make up this Ethiopian dish. The crunch of the greens is nice with the smooth, ginger-scented cheese.

1 carton (12 ounces) cottage cheese
2 tablespoons Ghee (page 23), margarine or butter
1 clove garlic, cut into halves
½ teaspoon ground cardamom
¼ teaspoon ground ginger
⅛ teaspoon ground cinnamon
⅛ teaspoon ground cloves
2 tablespoons finely chopped onion
1 green chile, seeded and finely chopped
1 to 2 teaspoons grated gingerroot
2 pounds fresh collard greens or spinach, coarsely chopped
2 tablespoons Ghee (page 23), margarine or butter

Mix cottage cheese, 2 tablespoons Ghee, the garlic, cardamom, ginger, cinnamon and cloves in medium bowl. Let stand 15 minutes; remove garlic. Cook onion, chile, gingerroot and collard greens in 2 tablespoons Ghee in Dutch oven until tender; drain. Serve collard greens over cottage cheese.   **6 servings**

PER SERVING: Calories 165; Protein 10 g; Carbohydrate 9 g; Fat 10 g; Cholesterol 10 mg; Sodium 420 mg

Apple-Cheese Oven Pancake

Apple-Cheese Oven Pancake

Have the apple filling ready as soon as the pancake is done. You have to work quickly, or the pancake will deflate before you fill it.

1 cup all-purpose flour
1 cup skim milk
¼ teaspoon salt
2 eggs
4 egg whites
1 tablespoon margarine
2 cups thinly sliced unpeeled tart cooking apples (about 2 medium)
2 tablespoons chopped fresh or 2 teaspoons freeze-dried chives
2 tablespoons sugar
¼ cup shredded low-fat cheddar cheese (1 ounce)

Heat oven to 450°. Spray rectangular baking dish, 13 × 9 × 2 inches, with nonstick cooking spray. Beat flour, milk, salt, eggs and egg whites until smooth; pour into dish. Bake about 15 to 20 minutes or until puffy and golden brown.

Meanwhile, heat margarine in 10-inch nonstick skillet over medium-high heat. Sauté apples and chives in margarine. Stir in sugar. Spoon apple mixture onto pancake. Sprinkle with cheese. Bake about 1 minute or until cheese is melted. **4 servings**

PER SERVING: Calories 295; Protein 14 g; Carbohydrate 43 g; Fat 7 g; Cholesterol 105 mg; Sodium 340 mg

Greek Oven Pancake

If you like Greek salads, you'll enjoy this twist on an oven pancake.

2 tablespoons reduced-calorie margarine
½ cup all-purpose flour
½ cup skim milk
¼ teaspoon Italian seasoning
¼ teaspoon salt
2 eggs
1 teaspoon reduced-calorie margarine
1 cup julienne strips zucchini (about 1 small)
1 cup crumbled feta cheese (5 ounces)
2 tablespoons chopped Greek olives

Heat oven to 425°. Heat 2 tablespoons margarine in square pan, 9 × 9 × 2 inches, in oven about 4 minutes or until hot and bubbly. Beat flour, milk, Italian seasoning, salt and eggs with hand beater until well blended. Pour into pan. Bake uncovered 20 to 25 minutes or until sides of pancake are puffed and deep golden brown.

Heat 1 teaspoon margarine in 1½-quart nonstick saucepan over medium heat. Cook zucchini about 2 minutes, stirring frequently, until crisp-tender. Carefully stir in cheese. Spoon onto center of pancake; sprinkle with olives. **4 servings**

PER SERVING: Calories 255; Protein 11 g; Carbohydrate 15 g; Fat 16 g; Cholesterol 140 mg; Sodium 650 mg

Gouda Cheese and Egg Casserole

Gouda is a Dutch cheese usually sold sealed in a brightly colored, waxy coating. This casserole is like a savory bread pudding, baked until the top is golden brown.

1¼ **cups half-and-half**
1¼ **cups soft bread crumbs**
1 **cup shredded Gouda cheese**
  (4 ounces)
¾ **teaspoon salt**
¼ **teaspoon pepper**
4 **eggs, slightly beaten**
Paprika

Heat oven to 325°. Mix all ingredients except paprika; pour into greased 1-quart casserole. Sprinkle with paprika. Bake uncovered until center is set, 45 to 50 minutes.   **4 servings**

PER SERVING: Calories 390; Protein 19 g; Carbohydrate 27 g; Fat 23 g; Cholesterol 270 mg; Sodium 1000 mg

Eggs and Spinach Casserole

½ **cup chopped onion (about 1 medium)**
1 **tablespoon reduced-calorie margarine**
3 **cups frozen shredded hash brown potatoes**
½ **teaspoon herb seasoning mix**
½ **teaspoon salt**
1 **package (10 ounces) frozen chopped spinach, thawed**
½ **cup shredded low-fat Swiss cheese (2 ounces)**
½ **cup low-fat sour cream**
6 **eggs**

Heat oven to 350°. Cook onion in margarine in 10-inch skillet over medium heat until softened, stirring occasionally. Stir in potatoes, seasoning mix, salt and spinach. Cook about 3 minutes, stirring constantly, just until potatoes are thawed. Stir in cheese and sour cream. Spread in ungreased square baking dish, 8 × 8 × 2 inches.

Make 6 indentations in potato mixture with back of spoon; break 1 egg into each indentation. Sprinkle with pepper if desired. Bake uncovered 30 to 35 minutes or until eggs are of desired doneness.   **6 servings**

PER SERVING: Calories 255; Protein 12 g; Carbohydrate 24 g; Fat 12 g; Cholesterol 230 mg; Sodium 320 mg

Impossible Chile-Cheese Pie

2 **cans (4 ounces each) chopped green chiles, drained**
4 **cups shredded Cheddar cheese (16 ounces)**
2 **cups milk**
1 **cup Bisquick®**
4 **eggs**

Heat oven to 425°. Grease pie plate, 10 × 1½ inches. Sprinkle chiles and cheese in pie plate. Place remaining ingredients in blender. Cover and blend on high speed about 15 seconds or until smooth. (Or beat remaining ingredients on high speed 1 minute.) Pour into pie plate. Bake 25 to 30 minutes or until knife inserted in center comes out clean. Cool 10 minutes.

8 servings

MICROWAVE DIRECTIONS: Do not grease pie plate. Decrease milk to 1½ cups. Prepare as directed. Elevate pie plate on inverted microwavable dinner plate in microwave oven. Microwave uncovered on medium-high (70%) 12 to 18 minutes, rotating pie plate ¼ turn every 6 minutes, until knife inserted in center comes out clean. Cool 10 minutes.

PER SERVING: Calories 360; Protein 20 g; Carbohydrate 14 g; Fat 25 g; Cholesterol 200 mg; Sodium 595 mg

Spinach-Cheese Pie

Phyllo is an elegant Greek contribution to the food world. It is flaky and, with a brushing of margarine or butter, browns very nicely. This pie makes a lovely appetizer when cut into bite-size pieces.

10 ounces fresh spinach (about 6 cups)
6 ounces feta cheese, crumbled (about 1 cup)
1 cup small-curd creamed cottage cheese
1 small onion, chopped (about ¼ cup)
2 tablespoons chopped parsley
1 tablespoon chopped fresh or 2 teaspoons dried dill weed
½ teaspoon salt
3 eggs, beaten
1 tablespoon margarine or butter, softened
½ package (16-ounce size) frozen phyllo leaves, thawed
½ cup margarine or butter, melted

Wash spinach; drain and chop. Cover and cook with just the water that clings to the leaves about 3 minutes or until tender; drain. Mix spinach, feta cheese, cottage cheese, onion, parsley, dill weed and salt. Stir spinach mixture into eggs.

Brush bottom and sides of rectangular baking dish, 11 × 7 × 1½ inches, with softened margarine. Unfold phyllo leaves. Remove 10 leaves; cut crosswise in half. (Cover completely with a sheet of waxed paper, then a damp towel to prevent drying. Wrap and refreeze remaining phyllo leaves.) Gently separate 1 half leaf. Place in baking dish, folding edges over to fit bottom of dish. Brush lightly with melted margarine. Repeat 9 times.

Heat oven to 350°. Spread spinach-egg mixture evenly over phyllo leaves. Layer 10 remaining phyllo leaves over filling, spreading each leaf with margarine and tucking in sides around edges to cover filling. Cut through top layer of phyllo leaves with sharp knife into 6 squares. Bake uncovered about 35 minutes or until golden. Let stand 10 minutes before cutting. Cut through scored lines to serve. **6 servings**

PER SERVING: Calories 430; Protein 17 g; Carbohydrate 135 mg; Fat 27 g; Cholesterol 135 mg; Sodium 1050 mg

Florentine Pie

Other types of rice such as brown and basmati work nicely for the shell.

1½ cups hot cooked rice
¼ cup grated Parmesan cheese
1 tablespoon chopped green onion tops
1 egg white
4 eggs
1 egg yolk
1 cup shredded Swiss cheese (4 ounces)
⅔ cup milk
¼ cup sliced green onions
¼ teaspoon salt
¼ teaspoon ground pepper
¼ teaspoon ground nutmeg
1 package (10 ounces) frozen chopped spinach, thawed and pressed dry

Heat oven to 325°. Grease pie plate, 9 × 1¼ inches. Mix rice, Parmesan cheese, 1 tablespoon green onion tops and the egg white with fork. Press mixture evenly on bottom and up side of pie plate (do not leave any holes). Bake 5 minutes.

Beat eggs and egg yolk with hand beater in medium bowl until very foamy. Stir in remaining ingredients. Pour into rice shell. Bake about 45 minutes or until knife inserted in center comes out clean. Serve with additional Parmesan cheese if desired. **6 servings**

PER SERVING: Calories 235; Protein 15 g; Carbohydrate 17 g; Fat 12 g; Cholesterol 245 mg; Sodium 490 mg

Mexican Strata

Mexican Strata

Whole-grain bread gives this do-ahead dish a nice hearty texture, but white bread can be used too.

8 slices whole-grain bread (crusts removed)
1½ cups shredded low-fat Cheddar cheese (6 ounces)
1 can (4 ounces) chopped green chiles, well drained
1 jar (2 ounces) sliced pimientos, well drained
1⅓ cups skim milk
¼ teaspoon ground cumin
6 egg whites or 1 cup cholesterol-free egg product

Spray square baking dish, 8 × 8 × 2 inches, with nonstick cooking spray. Place 4 slices bread in dish. Sprinkle with cheese, chiles and pimientos. Top with remaining bread. Beat remaining ingredients; pour over bread. Cover and refrigerate at least 2 hours but no longer than 24 hours.

Heat oven to 325°. Bake 1 hour to 1 hour 15 minutes or until set and top is golden brown. Let stand 10 minutes before serving.

4 servings

PER SERVING: Calories 320; Protein 25 g; Carbohydrate 32 g; Fat 9 g; Cholesterol 5 mg; Sodium 830 mg

Gouda Strata

2 tablespoons margarine or butter, softened
6 slices whole wheat bread
1 cup shredded Monterey Jack cheese (4 ounces)
1 cup shredded Gouda cheese (4 ounces)
1 small onion, finely chopped (about ¼ cup)
1 large clove garlic, crushed
1 teaspoon dry mustard
½ teaspoon salt
1½ cups milk
½ cup dry white wine or vegetable broth
¼ teaspoon red pepper sauce
4 eggs, slightly beaten

Heat oven to 325°. Spread margarine on 1 side of each slice bread. Cut each slice diagonally into 4 triangles. Place 8 triangles, buttered sides against sides and crust sides down, in ungreased square baking dish, 8 × 8 × 2 inches. Arrange 8 triangles, buttered sides down, on bottom of dish.

Mix cheeses, onion, garlic, mustard and salt; spread over bread. Arrange remaining 8 triangles, buttered sides up, on cheese mixture. Mix remaining ingredients; pour over bread. Bake uncovered about 1 hour 10 minutes or until knife inserted in center comes out clean. Let stand about 10 minutes before serving.

6 servings

PER SERVING: Calories 365; Protein 18 g; Carbohydrate 17 g; Fat 20 g; Cholesterol 170 mg; Sodium 690 mg

Baked Vegetable Omelet

Baked Vegetable Omelet

This baked omelet is especially nice when you are busy or would like to spend time preparing other parts of your meal.

**1 cup shredded pepper Jack cheese
    (4 ounces)
1½ cups chopped broccoli or 1 package
    (10 ounces) frozen chopped broccoli,
    thawed and drained
2 medium tomatoes, coarsely chopped
2 cups shredded Cheddar cheese
    (8 ounces)
1 cup milk
¼ cup all-purpose flour
½ teaspoon salt
3 eggs**

Layer pepper cheese, broccoli, tomatoes and Cheddar cheese in ungreased square baking dish, 8 × 8 × 2 inches. Beat milk, flour, salt and eggs until smooth; pour over cheese.

Bake uncovered in 350° oven until egg mixture is set, 40 to 45 minutes. Let stand 10 minutes before cutting. **6 servings**

PER SERVING: Calories 325; Protein 20 g; Carbohydrate 12 g; Fat 22 g; Cholesterol 170 mg; Sodium 600 mg

Cookware Confusion

Don't have the right size dish called for in a recipe? Don't despair—these helpful substitutions will prevent overfill as well as oven spills!

Casserole Size	Baking Pan or Dish Size
1½ quarts	11 × 7 × 1½ inches
2 quarts	8 × 8 × 2 inches
2½ quarts	9 × 9 × 2 inches
3 quarts	13 × 9 × 2 inches

Cheese-Stuffed Eggplant

Half of a smallish, stuffed eggplant is perfect for one serving. The addition of peanuts to the cheese filling adds crunch and enhances the protein value of the dish.

**2 small eggplants (about 1 pound each)
1 medium onion, chopped
2 cloves garlic, finely chopped
¼ cup olive or vegetable oil
1½ cups soft bread crumbs
1 cup salted peanuts
2 tablespoons chopped parsley
½ teaspoon salt
½ teaspoon ground marjoram
½ teaspoon ground oregano
2 medium tomatoes, cut into wedges
8 ounces mushrooms, thinly sliced
⅔ cup grated Parmesan cheese**

Cut eggplants lengthwise into halves. Cut out and cube enough eggplant from shells to measure about 4 cups, leaving a ½-inch wall on side and bottom of each shell; reserve shells. (To remove eggplant from shell easily, cut around side with a grapefruit knife.) Cook and stir eggplant cubes, onion and garlic in oil in 10-inch skillet over medium heat 5 minutes. Add remaining ingredients except reserved shells and cheese. Cover and cook over low heat 10 minutes.

Place eggplant shells in ungreased shallow pan; spoon peanut mixture into shells. Sprinkle cheese over filled shells. Cook uncovered in 350° oven until eggplant is tender, 30 to 40 minutes. **4 servings**

PER SERVING: Calories 660; Protein 23 g; Carbohydrate 57 g; Fat 38 g; Cholesterol 10 mg; Sodium 960 mg

Leek and Chevrè Pizza (page 81)

4

Pizzas, Sandwiches and More

Traditional Cheese Pizza

A variety of your favorite toppings can be added to the basic cheese pizza. For each 12-inch pizza, try one or more of the following: 1/4 cup sliced mushrooms, pitted ripe olives, chopped onions or chopped bell pepper.

Crust (right)
1 can (8 ounces) tomato sauce
1 teaspoon Italian seasoning
1 clove garlic, finely chopped
3 cups shredded mozzarella or Fontina cheese (12 ounces)
1 small onion, thinly sliced and separated into rings
1/4 cup grated Parmesan cheese

Place oven rack in lowest position. Grease 2 cookie sheets or 12-inch pizza pans. Heat oven to 425°. Prepare Crust. Mix tomato sauce, Italian seasoning and garlic. Divide dough in half. Pat each half into 11-inch circle on cookie sheet with floured fingers. Sprinkle with mozzarella cheese. Spoon tomato sauce mixture over cheese. Top with onion and Parmesan cheese. Bake one pizza at a time 15 to 20 minutes or until crust is golden brown. **12 servings**

Crust

1 package active dry yeast
1 cup warm water (105° to 115°)
2½ cups all-purpose flour
2 tablespoons olive or vegetable oil
1 teaspoon sugar
1 teaspoon salt

Dissolve yeast in warm water in medium bowl. Stir in remaining ingredients. Beat vigorously 20 strokes. Let rest 5 minutes.

PER SERVING: Calories 205; Protein 10 g; Carbohydrate 22 g; Fat 8 g; Cholesterol 20 mg; Sodium 400 mg

Pita Pizzas

Leek and Chèvre Pizza

Look for a slightly dry or crumbly cheese for this pizza. Fines herbes *can be purchased as a commercially prepared mixture, usually including chervil, parsley, tarragon and often chives.*

Pizza Dough (below)
1 teaspoon olive or vegetable oil
1 cup shredded mozzarella cheese
   (4 ounces)
1 cup thinly sliced leek (with tops)
1 cup well-drained chopped seeded tomato (about 1 medium)
½ teaspoon fines herbes
1 ounce chèvre cheese, chopped
1 large clove garlic, finely chopped
10 large pitted ripe olives, cut into
   fourths

Heat oven to 450°. Prepare Pizza Dough. Brush with oil; sprinkle with remaining ingredients. Bake until cheese is bubbly and crust is golden brown, 15 to 20 minutes. **6 servings**

Pizza Dough

1½ teaspoons active dry yeast (about
   half of ¼-ounce package)
⅓ cup warm water (105° to 115°)
½ teaspoon sugar
½ teaspoon salt
2 teaspoons olive or vegetable oil
1 cup whole wheat flour
1 tablespoon yellow or white cornmeal

Dissolve yeast in warm water in medium bowl. Stir in sugar, salt, oil and all of the flour except 2 tablespoons. (If dough is sticky, add remaining flour, 1 to 2 teaspoons at a time, until dough is easy to handle.) Turn onto surface dusted with cornmeal. Knead until smooth and elastic, about 2 minutes. Pat into 10-inch circle on cookie sheet, forming ½-inch rim.

PER SERVING: Calories 185; Protein 9 g; Carbohydrate 20 g; Fat 8 g; Cholesterol 15 mg; Sodium 370 mg

Pita Pizzas

4 whole wheat pita breads (4 inches in
   diameter)
¼ cup chopped onion (about 1 small)
1 small clove garlic, finely chopped
1 can (15½ ounces) great northern
   beans, drained and ¼ cup liquid
   reserved
2 tablespoons chopped fresh or 2 teaspoons dried basil leaves
1 large tomato, seeded and cut into
   ¼-inch pieces
1 large green bell pepper, cut into 16
   thin rings
1 cup shredded part-skim mozzarella
   cheese (4 ounces)

Heat oven to 425°. Cut each pita bread around edge in half with knife. Place in ungreased jelly roll pan, 15½ × 10½ × 1 inch. Bake uncovered about 5 minutes or just until crisp. Cook onion and garlic in reserved bean liquid in 10-inch nonstick skillet over medium heat about 5 minutes, stirring occasionally. Stir in beans; heat through.

Place bean mixture and basil in blender or food processor. Cover and blend or process until smooth. Spread about 2 tablespoons bean mixture on each pita bread half. Top each with tomato, bell pepper and cheese. Bake in jelly roll pan 5 to 7 minutes or until cheese is melted. **4 servings**

PER SERVING: Calories 415; Protein 23 g; Carbohydrate 70 g; Fat 7 g; Cholesterol 20 mg; Sodium 420 mg

Vegetable Pizza with Wheat Germ Crust

Wheat Germ Crust (below)
1 cup shredded Monterey Jack cheese (4 ounces)
1 can (8 ounces) pizza sauce
1 small zucchini, thinly sliced
1 cup sliced mushrooms or 1 jar (4.5 ounces) sliced mushrooms, drained
3 green onions sliced
1 cup shredded Cheddar cheese (4 ounces)

Heat oven to 425°. Prepare Wheat Germ Crust; sprinkle with Monterey Jack cheese. Drizzle with pizza sauce. Arrange zucchini, mushrooms and onions on pizza sauce; sprinkle with Cheddar cheese. Bake until crust is golden brown, about 20 minutes. Garnish with alfalfa sprouts and avocado slices if desired.   **6 servings**

Wheat Germ Crust

2 cups Bisquick®
¼ cup wheat germ
⅔ cup cold water

Mix Bisquick, wheat germ and water until soft dough forms; beat vigorously 20 strokes. Using floured fingers, pat dough into 11-inch circle on greased cookie sheet, building up ½-inch edge. Or pat in greased 12-inch pizza pan.

PER SERVING: Calories 365; Protein 14 g; Carbohydrate 32 g; Fat 20 g; Cholesterol 40 mg; Sodium 970 mg

Swiss Cheese and Vegetables in Pita Breads

1 cup shredded Swiss cheese (4 ounces)
½ cup thinly sliced cauliflowerets
¼ cup mayonnaise or salad dressing
1 teaspoon chopped fresh or ½ teaspoon dried dill weed
½ teaspoon salt
1 medium tomato, chopped
1 small zucchini or carrot, shredded
3 pita breads (6-inch diameter), cut into halves
Salad greens

Mix all ingredients except pita breads and salad greens. Separate pita breads along cut sides to form pockets. Arrange salad greens and vegetable mixture in pockets.   **6 servings**

PER SERVING: Calories 260; Protein 10 g; Carbohydrate 26 g; Fat 13 g; Cholesterol 20 mg; Sodium 480 mg

Baked Eggplant Sandwiches

3 tablespoons vegetable oil
1 medium eggplant (about 1¼ pounds)
6 tablespoons pizza sauce
6 slices mozzarella cheese (about 4 ounces)
2 eggs
¼ cup milk
½ cup Italian-style dry bread crumbs
¼ cup chopped parsley

Heat oven to 400°. Brush 1 tablespoon oil on bottom of rectangular pan, 13 × 9 × 2 inches. Cut eggplant into twelve ½-inch slices. Spoon about 1 tablespoon pizza sauce onto each of 6 eggplant slices. Top each with 1 slice cheese (cut or fold cheese, if necessary, to fit) and with remaining eggplant slices.

Beat eggs and milk. Mix bread crumbs and parsley in shallow dish. Dip each sandwich into egg mixture, then into crumb mixture, turning to coat both sides. Press crumb mixture into and around edges to coat entire sandwich.

Place sandwiches in pan. Drizzle with remaining oil. Cover pan with aluminum foil. Bake 20 minutes. Remove foil and turn sandwiches. Bake 15 to 30 minutes longer or until sandwiches are golden brown and eggplant is tender.

6 servings

PER SERVING: Calories 215; Protein 8 g; Carbohydrate 15 g; Fat 14 g; Cholesterol 105 mg; Sodium 250 mg

Grilled Fruit-and-Cheese Sandwiches

For a change of pace, use flavored cream cheese for the regular cream cheese and Swiss cheese in place of the Monterey Jack.

1 cup shredded Monterey Jack cheese (4 ounces)
⅓ cup crumbled blue cheese
2 tablespoons milk
1 package (3 ounces) cream cheese, softened
8 one-quarter-inch slices sourdough bread
1 small ripe pear, thinly sliced
1 small all-purpose apple, thinly sliced
Margarine or butter, softened

Mix Monterey Jack cheese, blue cheese, milk and cream cheese. Spread about 2 tablespoons on each slice bread. Place pear and apple slices on cheese mixture on 4 slices bread. Place remaining slices bread, cheese side down, on pear and apple slices. Spread tops with margarine.

Place sandwiches, margarine sides down, in skillet. Spread tops with margarine. Cook uncovered over medium heat about 5 minutes or until golden brown. Turn and cook 2 to 3 minutes longer or until golden brown. **4 servings**

PER SERVING: Calories 445; Protein 14 g; Carbohydrate 27 g; Fat 32 g; Cholesterol 35 mg; Sodium 660 mg

Whole Wheat Ratatouille Calzone

Whole Wheat Ratatouille Calzone

Whole wheat adds extra goodness to this Italian classic.

Whole Wheat Calzone Dough (right)
2 teaspoons olive or vegetable oil
2 cups ½-inch cubes eggplant (about ½ pound)
1 cup sliced zucchini (about ⅔ medium)
½ cup coarsely chopped green bell pepper (about 1 small)
2 teaspoons chopped fresh or ½ teaspoon dried basil leaves
1 teaspoon chopped fresh or ¼ teaspoon dried oregano leaves
½ teaspoon salt
¼ teaspoon pepper
2 medium tomatoes, cut into eighths
1 small onion, thinly sliced
1 clove garlic, crushed
1 cup shredded part-skim mozzarella cheese (4 ounces)
2 tablespoons grated Parmesan cheese
1 egg white, beaten

Heat oven to 375°. Prepare Whole Wheat Calzone Dough.

Heat oil in 10-inch nonstick skillet over medium heat. Cook remaining ingredients except cheeses and egg white in oil uncovered, stirring frequently, until vegetables are tender and liquid is evaporated.

Spray cookie sheet with nonstick cooking spray. Divide Calzone Dough into 4 equal pieces. Pat each into 8-inch circle on lightly floured surface, turning dough over occasionally to coat lightly with flour. Top half of each circle with about ¾ cup vegetable mixture to within 1 inch of edge. Sprinkle cheeses over vegetable mixture. Fold dough over vegetable mixture; fold edge up and pinch securely to seal. Place on cookie sheet. Brush with egg white. Bake about 25 minutes or until golden brown.   **4 servings**

Whole Wheat Calzone Dough

1 package active dry yeast
¾ cup warm water (105° to 115°)
1 tablespoon sugar
¾ teaspoon salt
1 tablespoon olive or vegetable oil
1¾ to 2¼ cups whole wheat flour

Dissolve yeast in warm water in large bowl. Stir in sugar, salt, oil and 1 cup of the flour. Beat until smooth. Mix in enough remaining flour to make dough easy to handle.

Turn dough onto lightly floured surface. Knead about 5 minutes or until smooth and elastic. Cover with bowl and let rest 5 minutes.

PER SERVING: Calories 400; Protein 19 g; Carbohydrate 58 g; Fat 12 g; Cholesterol 20 mg; Sodium 890 mg

Brie and Cucumber on Rye

½ **seedless cucumber**
8 **ounces Brie cheese, cut into ¼-inch**
   pieces
¼ **cup finely chopped green onions**
¼ **cup oil-and-vinegar dressing**
¾ **teaspoon chopped fresh or ¼ tea-**
   spoon dried dill weed
4 **teaspoons margarine or butter,**
   softened
4 **slices rye bread**
Salad greens

Cut cucumber lengthwise in half. Cut each half into thin slices. Toss cucumber, cheese, onions, dressing and dill weed.

Spread 1 teaspoon margarine on each slice bread. Top with salad greens. Spoon cheese mixture onto greens. Garnish each sandwich with fresh dill weed if desired. **4 servings**

ZUCCHINI AND CREAM CHEESE SANDWICHES: Substitute 1 medium zucchini for the English cucumber and 1 package (8 ounces) cream cheese for the Brie cheese.

PER SERVING: Calories 370; Protein 15 g; Carbohydrate 14 g; Fat 29 g; Cholesterol 60 mg; Sodium 720 mg

Mediterranean Sandwiches

Throughout the Middle East, hummus, made from garbanzo beans, is common. It makes a wonderful sandwich and also can be served as a delicious dip.

1 **can (15 ounces) garbanzo beans**
½ **cup sesame seed**
1 **clove garlic, cut in half**
3 **tablespoons lemon juice**
¼ **teaspoon salt**
16 **one-half-inch diagonal slices French**
   bread
2 **tablespoons chopped fresh cilantro**
½ **cup chopped bell pepper**
½ **medium cucumber, thinly sliced**
1 **cup alfalfa sprouts**

Drain beans, reserving ⅓ cup liquid. Place reserved bean liquid, the sesame seed and garlic in blender or food processor. Cover and blend on high speed, or process, until mixed. Add beans, lemon juice and salt. Cover and blend on high speed, or process, scraping sides, if necessary, until of uniform consistency.

Spread about 2 tablespoons bean mixture on each slice bread. Sprinkle cilantro and bell pepper on 8 of the slices bread. Top with cucumber slices and alfalfa sprouts. Top with remaining slices bread. **4 servings**

PER SERVING: Calories 380; Protein 15 g; Carbohydrate 53 g; Fat 13 g; Cholesterol 0 mg; Sodium 700 mg

Leek and Mushroom Tart

This tart is also nice when you use a prepared crust. Follow package directions for baking.

Pastry for 9-inch One-Crust Pie (below)
3 tablespoons margarine or butter
2 cups sliced leeks, (about ½ pound)
1 cup coarsely chopped shiitake or other fresh mushrooms
1 cup shredded white Cheddar or Cheddar cheese (4 ounces)
¾ cup shredded mozzarella cheese (3 ounces)
⅔ cup milk
½ teaspoon salt
½ teaspoon ground nutmeg
3 eggs

Prepare and bake Pastry.

Reduce oven temperature to 350°. Heat margarine in 10-inch skillet over medium heat. Cook leeks and mushrooms in margarine about 5 minutes. Spread in cooled crust. Sprinkle with cheeses. Beat remaining ingredients. Pour over cheeses. Bake about 35 minutes or until set. **6 servings**

Pastry for 9-Inch One-Crust Pie

½ cup plus 1 tablespoon shortening or ⅓ cup lard
1 cup all-purpose flour
¼ teaspoon salt
2 to 3 tablespoons cold water

Heat oven to 475°. Cut shortening into flour and salt until particles are size of small peas. Sprinkle in water, 1 tablespoon at a time, tossing with fork until all flour is moistened and pastry almost cleans side of bowl (1 to 2 teaspoons water can be added if necessary).

Gather pastry into a ball. Shape into flattened round on lightly floured cloth-covered board.

Roll pastry 2 inches larger than inverted 9 × 1-inch tart pan, or 9 × 1¼-inch pie plate, with floured cloth-covered rolling pin. Fold pastry into fourths; place in pan. Unfold and ease into pan, pressing firmly against bottom and side.

Trim overhanging edge of pastry 1 inch from rim of pan. Fold and roll pastry under, even with pan; flute.

Prick bottom and side thoroughly with fork. Bake 8 to 10 minutes or until light brown; cool.

PER SERVING: Calories 360; Protein 12 g; Carbohydrate 21 g; Fat 26 g; Cholesterol 160 mg; Sodium 610 mg

Easy Three-Cheese Quiche

1 cup shredded Cheddar cheese (4 ounces)
1 cup shredded mozzarella cheese (4 ounces)
1 cup shredded Monterey Jack cheese (4 ounces)
1 medium onion, chopped (about ½ cup)
2 tablespoons all-purpose flour
4 eggs
1 cup milk
½ teaspoon salt
½ teaspoon dry mustard
½ teaspoon Worcestershire sauce
2 medium tomatoes, sliced

Mix cheeses, onion and flour. Spread in greased pie plate, 10 × 1½ inches, or quiche dish, 9 × 1½ inches. Beat eggs slightly; beat in milk, salt, mustard and Worcestershire sauce. Pour over cheese mixture. Bake uncovered in 350° oven until set, 35 to 40 minutes. Let stand 10 minutes; arrange tomato slices around edge of pie, overlapping slices slightly. **8 servings**

PER SERVING: Calories 225; Protein 15 g; Carbohydrate 7 g; Fat 15 g; Cholesterol 150 mg; Sodium 440 mg

Rice Noodles with Peanut Sauce

2 quarts water
½ cup creamy peanut butter
2 tablespoons soy sauce
1 teaspoon grated gingerroot
½ teaspoon crushed red pepper
½ cup water or chicken broth
8 ounces uncooked rice stick noodles
4 ounces bean sprouts
1 red bell pepper, cut into fourths and sliced thinly crosswise
2 green onions, sliced
2 tablespoons chopped cilantro, if desired

Heat 2 quarts water to boiling. Mix peanut butter, soy sauce, gingerroot and red pepper until smooth. Gradually stir in ½ cup water. Break noodles in half and pull apart slightly while dropping into boiling water. Cook uncovered 1 minute; drain. Rinse in cold water; drain. Place noodles in large bowl. Add peanut butter mixture, bean sprouts, bell pepper and green onions; toss. Sprinkle with cilantro.

4 servings

PER SERVING: Calories 390; Protein 14 g; Carbohydrate 43 g; Fat 18 g; Cholesterol 0 mg; Sodium 670 mg

Rigatoni with Pesto Sauce

This Pesto Sauce can be frozen up to six months. Let stand at room temperature about four hours or until thawed.

Pesto Sauce (below)
1 package (16 ounces) rigatoni

Prepare Pesto Sauce. Cook rigatoni as directed on package; drain. Toss sauce and rigatoni until well coated. Sprinkle with grated Parmesan cheese if desired. **8 servings**

Pesto Sauce

2 cups firmly packed fresh basil leaves
¾ cup grated Parmesan cheese
¾ cup olive oil
2 tablespoons pine nuts
2 tablespoons chopped fresh oregano leaves
4 cloves garlic

Place all ingredients in blender. Cover and blend on medium speed about 3 minutes, stopping blender frequently to scrape sides, until smooth.

PER SERVING: Calories 450; Protein 12 g; Carbohydrate 45 g; Fat 26 g; Cholesterol 60 mg; Sodium 155 mg

Herbed Tricolor Pasta

**8 ounces uncooked vegetable-flavored
 rotini (about 3 cups)**
**2 teaspoons chopped fresh or ½ tea-
 spoon dried savory leaves, crushed**
¼ cup whipping (heavy) cream
**6 ounces herb-flavored Havarti cheese,
 shredded**
2 small summer squash, thinly sliced
Coarsely ground pepper

Cook rotini as directed on package—except add savory to water; drain.

Stir in whipping cream, cheese and squash until cheese is melted. Arrange on platter; sprinkle with pepper. Garnish with fresh savory leaves if desired. **6 servings**

PER SERVING: Calories 395; Protein 16 g; Carbohydrate 47 g; Fat 16 g; Cholesterol 105 mg; Sodium 470 mg

Double Cheese Tortellini

**2 cans (16 ounces each) stewed
 tomatoes**
½ teaspoon dried oregano leaves
**1 package (7.05 ounces) uncooked dried
 cheese-filled tortellini**
**1 cup shredded Cheddar cheese
 (4 ounces)**

Heat tomatoes and oregano to boiling in 3-quart saucepan; stir in tortellini. Heat to boiling; reduce heat.

Boil gently, stirring occasionally, until tortellini is of desired doneness, 20 to 25 minutes. (Add 1 to 2 tablespoons water during last 5 minutes of cooking, if necessary, to prevent sticking.) Top each serving with ¼ cup cheese.

4 servings

PER SERVING: Calories 490; Protein 24 g; Carbohydrate 45 g; Fat 24 g; Cholesterol 170 mg; Sodium 1190 mg

Scrambled Eggs in Buns

6 unsliced hamburger buns
¼ cup margarine or butter, melted
6 tablespoons shredded Cheddar cheese
8 eggs
½ cup milk
1 teaspoon salt
¼ teaspoon pepper
2 tablespoons margarine or butter

Cut a hole about 2 inches in diameter in top of each bun; scoop out the inside, leaving about a ¼-inch wall. Place on ungreased cookie sheet. Brush insides of buns with ¼ cup melted margarine; spoon 1 tablespoon shredded cheese into each. Cook in 350° oven until buns are slightly crisp, 10 to 15 minutes.

Mix eggs, milk, salt and pepper with fork until uniform in color. Heat 2 tablespoons margarine in 10-inch skillet just until hot enough to sizzle a drop of water. Pour egg mixture into skillet. As mixture begins to set at bottom and side, gently lift cooked portions with spatula so that thin uncooked portions can flow to bottom. Avoid constant stirring. Cook until eggs are thickened throughout but still moist. Spoon eggs into warm buns. Garnish with olives if desired.

6 servings

PER SERVING: Calories 365; Protein 14 g; Carbohydrate 25 g; Fat 23 g; Cholesterol 290 mg; Sodium 840 mg

Macaroni and Cheese with Green Chiles

Fruit Chimichangas

Any flour tortilla that is stuffed, folded like a burrito and deep fried may be called a chimichanga. This sweet-tart apricot version is lighter (it's baked instead of fried in oil) and makes a very satisfying brunch dish or light supper.

Apricot Sauce (right)
1 package (8 ounces) cream cheese, softened
½ cup ricotta cheese
¼ cup sugar
1 teaspoon grated orange peel
6 flour tortillas (8 inches in diameter), warmed
¼ cup apricot preserves
1 egg, beaten
2 tablespoons margarine or butter, softened
1 cup sliced apricots

Prepare Apricot Sauce; reserve. Heat oven to 500°. Mix cream cheese, ricotta cheese, sugar and orange peel thoroughly. Spoon about ¼ cup mixture onto center of each tortilla; top with 1 tablespoon preserves.

Fold one end of tortilla up about 1 inch over mixture; fold right and left sides over folded end, overlapping. Fold remaining end down; brush edges with egg to seal. Brush each chimichanga with margarine.

Place seam sides down in ungreased jelly roll pan, 15½ × 10½ × 1 inch. Bake until chimichangas begin to brown and filling is hot, 8 to 10 minutes. Serve with apricots and Apricot Sauce. **6 servings**

Apricot Sauce

½ cup apricot jam
¼ cup dried apricots, finely chopped
¼ cup dry white wine or apple juice
1 tablespoon honey
1 teaspoon Worcestershire sauce

Heat all ingredients over low heat, stirring occasionally, until jam is melted.

PER SERVING: Calories 525; Protein 10 g; Carbohydrate 69 g; Fat 23 g; Cholesterol 85 mg; Sodium 380 mg

Macaroni and Cheese with Green Chiles

3 cups uncooked shell macaroni (about 12 ounces)
1 cup half-and-half
½ cup shredded Cheddar cheese (2 ounces)
½ cup sliced ripe olives
½ cup chopped mild green chiles or 1 can (4 ounces) chopped green chiles, drained
½ cup chopped red bell pepper or 1 jar (2 ounces) diced pimientos, drained
½ teaspoon salt

Cook macaroni as directed on package; drain. Stir in remaining ingredients. Cook over low heat, stirring occasionally, until cheese is melted and sauce is hot, about 5 minutes.

6 servings

PER SERVING: Calories 355; Protein 12 g; Carbohydrate 54 g; Fat 10 g; Cholesterol 25 mg; Sodium 780 mg

Cheese-Stuffed Chiles

Poblano chiles are the perfect size for stuffing, and though they are somewhat less sturdy when they have been blistered and peeled, they will not fall to pieces. These Mexican chiles are filled with a mixture of two cheeses, then coated with crumbs and fried.

8 poblano chiles, 3½ to 4½ inches long
8 tablespoons shredded Monterey Jack cheese (about 2 ounces)
8 tablespoons shredded Cheddar cheese (about 2 ounces)
½ cup dry bread crumbs
4 eggs, separated
¼ teaspoon salt
¼ teaspoon cream of tartar
Vegetable oil
Mexican Sauce (right)
Sour cream
Chopped cilantro

Set oven control to broil or 550°. Place chiles on rack in broiler pan. Broil with tops 4 to 5 inches from heat, turning frequently, until skins blister all around, up to 15 minutes. Place in plastic bags and close tightly; let stand 20 minutes. Carefully peel chiles, starting at stem end. Cut lengthwise slit down side of each chile. Carefully remove seeds and membranes; rinse. Fill each chile with 1 tablespoon Monterey Jack cheese and 1 tablespoon Cheddar cheese; coat with bread crumbs. Cover and refrigerate 20 minutes.

Beat egg whites, salt and cream of tartar in large bowl until stiff. Beat egg yolks until thick and lemon-colored, about 5 minutes; fold into egg whites. Heat 1 to 1½ inches oil to 375° in Dutch oven. Coat each chile again with bread crumbs; dip into egg mixture. Fry 1 or 2 chiles at a time, turning once, until puffy and golden brown, about 4 minutes. Drain chiles; keep warm in oven.

Prepare Mexican Sauce; pour over chiles. Garnish with sour cream and cilantro.

8 servings

Mexican Sauce

1 medium onion, chopped
½ medium green pepper, chopped
1 clove garlic, finely chopped
1 tablespoon vegetable oil
2 cups chopped ripe tomatoes*
¼ to ½ cup chopped green chiles
½ teaspoon sugar
⅛ teaspoon salt
5 drops red pepper sauce

Cook and stir onion, green pepper and garlic in oil in 2-quart saucepan until green pepper is tender, about 5 minutes. Stir in remaining ingredients. Heat to boiling; reduce heat. Simmer uncovered until slightly thickened, about 15 minutes.

*1 can (16 ounces) tomatoes (with liquid) can be substituted for the ripe tomatoes. Break up tomatoes with fork.

PER SERVING: Calories 270; Protein 9 g; Carbohydrate 13 g; Fat 20 g; Cholesterol 140 mg; Sodium 570 mg

Egg-Bean Sandwiches

1 can (16 ounces) refried beans
3 English muffins, split and toasted
¾ cup shredded Cheddar cheese (about
    6 ounces)
2 medium tomatoes, thinly sliced
6 eggs
¼ cup chopped green onions

Heat beans until hot; spread muffin halves with beans. Sprinkle cheese over beans; arrange tomatoes on cheese. Heat water (1½ to 2 inches) to boiling; reduce to simmer. Break each egg into measuring cup or saucer; holding cup close to water's surface, slip 1 egg at a time into water. Cook until of desired doneness, 3 to 5 minutes. Remove eggs from water with slotted spoon. Place eggs on tomatoes; sprinkle with onions.   **6 servings**

PER SERVING: Calories 280; Protein 17 g; Carbohydrate 30 g; Fat 11 g; Cholesterol 230 mg; Sodium 620 mg

Steaming Fresh Vegetables

Steaming not only retains the flavor, shape and texture of vegetables, it's a healthy way of cooking. No added fat is necessary, and water-soluble vitamins aren't lost in cooking water. A large saucepan with a tight-fitting lid and a steamer basket or rack is all that you need to steam vegetables.

• Wash, trim and peel vegetables as necessary. Leave vegetables whole or cut into pieces of the same size for even cooking.

• Place steamer basket in ½ inch water in saucepan (water should not touch bottom of basket). Place vegetables in basket. Cover tightly and heat to boiling; reduce heat. Cook until vegetables are of desired doneness.

• For longer-cooking vegetables, add more hot water, if necessary, to prevent water from boiling away.

METRIC CONVERSION GUIDE

U.S. UNITS	CANADIAN METRIC	AUSTRALIAN METRIC
Volume		
1/4 teaspoon	1 mL	1 ml
1/2 teaspoon	2 mL	2 ml
1 teaspoon	5 mL	5 ml
1 tablespoon	15 mL	20 ml
1/4 cup	50 mL	60 ml
1/3 cup	75 mL	80 ml
1/2 cup	125 mL	125 ml
2/3 cup	150 mL	170 ml
3/4 cup	175 mL	190 ml
1 cup	250 mL	250 ml
1 quart	1 liter	1 liter
1 1/2 quarts	1.5 liter	1.5 liter
2 quarts	2 liters	2 liters
2 1/2 quarts	2.5 liters	2.5 liters
3 quarts	3 liters	3 liters
4 quarts	4 liters	4 liters
Weight		
1 ounce	30 grams	30 grams
2 ounces	55 grams	60 grams
3 ounces	85 grams	90 grams
4 ounces (1/4 pound)	115 grams	125 grams
8 ounces (1/2 pound)	225 grams	225 grams
16 ounces (1 pound)	455 grams	500 grams
1 pound	455 grams	1/2 kilogram

Measurements		**Temperatures**	
Inches	Centimeters	Fahrenheit	Celsius
1	2.5	32°	0°
2	5.0	212°	100°
3	7.5	250°	120°
4	10.0	275°	140°
5	12.5	300°	150°
6	15.0	325°	160°
7	17.5	350°	180°
8	20.5	375°	190°
9	23.0	400°	200°
10	25.5	425°	220°
11	28.0	450°	230°
12	30.5	475°	240°
13	33.0	500°	260°
14	35.5		
15	38.0		

NOTE
The recipes in this cookbook have not been developed or tested using metric measures. When converting recipes to metric, some variations in quality may be noted.

Index

Page numbers in *italics* indicate photographs.